Glue Ear

An essential guide for teachers, parents and health professionals

Dr Lindsay Peer, CBE, C. Psychol

 **David Fulton** Publishers

David Fulton Publishers Ltd
The Chiswick Centre, 414 Chiswick High Road, London W4 5TF

www.fultonpublishers.co.uk
www.onestopeducation.co.uk

First published in Great Britain by David Fulton Publishers 2005

10 9 8 7 6 5 4 3 2 1

Note: The right of Lindsay Peer to be identified as the author of this work has been asserted by her in accordance with the Copyright, Designs and Patents Act 1988.

David Fulton Publishers is a division of Granada Learning Limited, part of ITV plc.

British Library Cataloguing in Publication Data
A catalogue record for this book is available from the British Library.

ISBN 1-84312-352-5

Typeset by FiSH Books, London
Printed and bound in Great Britain

Contents

Acknowledgements and dedication

I have worked in the field of education since 1974 and have learned a great deal from colleagues, students and parents. Dyslexia has taken me across the world to speak to and work with parents, educators, health workers and policy makers who are struggling with the same issues as those we encounter here in the UK. These people too have been more than generous by sharing with me their knowledge, concerns and wisdom. I thank them all.

I thank too my husband Michael for his patience, support – and proof-reading skills! Also my son for the excellent illustrations he has submitted to this book.

My greatest teachers have been my own children. This book is dedicated to them – three wonderful young people, successes each one in their own way. Each one dyslexic and a sufferer of glue ear.

Maya – a highly successful recruitment consultant
Yaniv – half-way to becoming an architect
Dana – about to read social psychology. 'I want to do for primates mum, what you have done for dyslexic children!' There is no answer to that!

We have had some challenging moments, as well as some highly amusing ones; how they used to muddle up their language!

'Can I have some cubumber please?'
'Why are prunes dangerous?' She meant piranhas!
'Please can I have lavina ice cream?'
'I left my bike in the karp.'

We have laughed and cried together over the years. With determination and understanding we learned that no-one and nothing must ever hold anyone back from fulfilling their dreams.

Educators, health professionals and parents all need to be aware of the impact that glue ear and/or dyslexia may have on the child. Empowerment on the part of parents, transfer of information to and from health professionals, and a co-operative working relationship between home and school will create an atmosphere in which these children will thrive.

Preface

I have endeavoured to provide in this book a practical guide for teachers, health professionals and parents.

Teachers – because many have not been told about the impact that this common condition can have on children's learning – in both primary and secondary phases. Greater knowledge and appropriate teaching techniques will enable teachers to make better provision for these pupils, resulting in fewer behaviour problems and improved academic achievements.

Health professionals (health visitors, GPs, school nurses, ENT consultants) – because they do not always understand the (sometimes long-term) impact of glue ear on a child's learning. If they could explain to parents and teachers about the possible difficulties created by the condition, better support could be put in place.

Parents – because they need to understand why their child may not respond when told to do something, why school reports may be less than glowing, why the child may have no friends … and be able to share this understanding with other family members and teachers.

I hope that the information and guidance contained in this book will help towards creating a greater understanding of the condition, and give support to those who most need it.

Lindsay Peer can be reached through her website: www.peergordonassociates.co.uk

Introduction

Glue ear is a very common condition among young children. It is thought that 15–20 per cent of children between two and five years of age are likely to have glue ear at any one time. (Older children can also have glue ear, though this is less common.)

It is basically an inflammation of the middle ear, sometimes accompanied by a sticky discharge which gives the condition its common name – 'Glue ear'; the medical name is otitis media. The episodes are usually short, but may be recurring and result in some degree of hearing loss.

Glue ear tends to be a fluctuating problem, meaning that sometimes the child may hear better than at others. One month the child may function well and the next be very poorly; this is very confusing to parents and other adults working with the child, as behaviour and reactions tend to change rapidly. The condition and people's responses to sufferers both during and after bouts can be very disruptive indeed in terms of a child's self-perception, emotional development and education. No wonder children look confused when people shout at them, telling them to attend and concentrate harder as they had done in the previous week!

Young children who have severe bouts of glue ear may not receive the input necessary for normal development of language and literacy skills and their sense of balance (vestibular skill) may also be affected. The presence of glue ear, at a time when auditory and vestibular skills are developing rapidly, may result in symptoms of dyslexia and my research has identified a significant link between these two conditions.

The issue of behaviour is an important consideration. When children cannot hear well and language is spoken too fast for them to understand, life can appear to be passing them by and this can be frightening. A child's response to this can be to withdraw, or to behave in an unconventional way. Social interaction with peers can be difficult and coupled with constantly feeling unwell, can lead to emotional instability for some children affected with glue ear.

Children with glue ear difficulties and those at risk of dyslexia can be identified at a very young age indeed, long before they start to acquire written literacy skills. Given appropriate provision and empathy as early as possible, they can go on to achieve beyond anyone's expectations. Those who are identified at an older age need to have appropriate support and intervention put in place as soon as their difficulties are recognised. As a result:

- behaviour will improve;
- academic achievement will be raised; and
- parents will be comforted knowing that their children are being taught appropriately.

1 What does glue ear mean to children and their families?

During my research into glue ear and its link with dyslexia, I spoke to many parents about their experiences. I have used five families' stories in this chapter to 'set the scene' for the rest of the book.

Family 1:

Our little Sara has had grommets inserted – at last! So far so good – she was instantly transformed, just as you had predicted. Went in to the hospital at 7.00am and out at 2.00pm a much happier toddler. In the hospital, far from being fearful of newly-heard sounds as we had been warned, she delighted in hearing the loo flushing and wanted to hear it again and again! The surgeon said that he was reluctant to take out adenoids in one so young (15 months) but might have to in future and will review. The operation was very necessary as the glue was compacted and distorting the bones. But when they removed the glue, the bones popped back into place...phew!

Thank you so much for the advice you gave us. Now let's hope the operation remains successful, the grommets stay in, there is no infection and all is well.

Family 2:

We have a son who was born with glue ear. He failed every hearing test at his health checks and suffered ear infection after ear infection. At the age of 13 months he was referred to the Ear, Nose and Throat Hospital in London for grommets to be inserted; this procedure was repeated when he was three years old. He then had a tonsillectomy and adenoidectomy at the age of seven.

We battled all through infant and junior school because we felt that he had difficulty with reading and writing. Unfortunately we were told at the time that we were just comparing him to his older brother who was a very able child. Things got much better once he got to secondary school thanks to a very dedicated Special Needs Team and he had weekly help until the age of 14 when the funding ran out. Thankfully, one of the learning support teachers continued working with him when she could and last year managed to get an educational psychologist's assessment. At the age of 16 he was finally diagnosed as being dyslexic. He had extra time in his GCSEs and achieved ten passes at grades C–A*. He is now in the sixth form and the school have just given him a laptop for his assignments.

I am sure that you have heard of many children like our son, but sometimes we felt like we were on our own fighting for what he needed. He was never badly behaved or disruptive at school and somebody once said to us that if he had been, we would have had the help he needed much quicker. He has had no problem with maths or practical subjects and is about to take the Grade 7 exam on the cello, so teachers haven't always seen the struggle he has had with writing specifically. He now has the spelling age of 9.8 years and a reading age of 15; so long as he has a computer with a spellchecker he can survive well. But it has been a long battle getting to this point.

Family 3:

My son had tubes put in at the age of four years and just this year at age 11, we had him tested and discovered he is dyslexic. We have researched our family histories and so far have not uncovered any relative who is/was dyslexic. Please could you send information to us on this subject. I want to give it to my child's paediatrician – who is part of a health co-operative.

Family 4:

We have a daughter aged 11 and a son aged seven. She was diagnosed with glue ear when two years old, but as it was intermittent she was not fitted with grommets until she started school. The speech impediments she had had resolved themselves immediately, but she really struggled with school work and her lack of ability to spell is still a problem to this day. Now at comprehensive school, she is proving that she has ability but has to work ten times harder than her peers to keep up with written work and learning by rote is really hard for her. We were fortunate that a part-time teacher at her school was also the SENCo at my son's school. Because of her problems, they have been monitoring his progress carefully and giving help almost before it is needed, which is wonderful. He too was diagnosed with glue ear almost by accident. No-one had told me that as his sister had it, it was almost a forgone conclusion that he would suffer too. I can't help wondering if her problems would have been avoided if she'd had grommets fitted earlier? Could my son's condition not have been picked up sooner if I had known he was almost certain to get it? I would not have ignored his speech problems for so long, that is for sure.

Family 5:

I am a very anxious parent of a child who is struggling with specific learning difficulties. She has dyslexic traits and as a toddler had grommets fitted because she had glue ear. Please could you help us?

2 Symptoms, treatments and guidance for parents

What is glue ear?

Glue ear is a very common condition that affects young children under the age of eight, but older children can also be affected. It can affect one or both ears. It is a condition in which a sticky fluid, glue-like in texture, builds up inside the ear. As it builds up, it blocks the airways needed for good hearing.

For many children the condition clears up quickly, but others have a persistent problem which may lead to long-term hearing difficulties. Some children go on to suffer developmental delay in speech and language and some suffer from symptoms consistent with dyslexia.

The medical name for glue ear is otitis media (with or without effusion). That means that some children have the problem and you can see it, as the glue tends to leak from the ear(s) from time to time. Other children do not have this external sign at all; they are harder to identify as you cannot see the physical symptoms of the problem.

How does glue ear affect hearing?

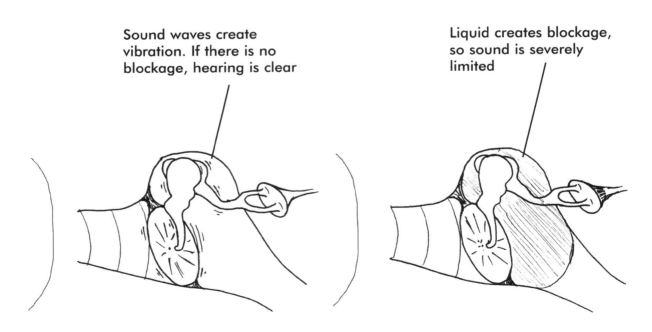

Sound waves create vibration. If there is no blockage, hearing is clear

Liquid creates blockage, so sound is severely limited

Figure 1a Healthy ear

Figure 1b Unhealthy ear

Hearing takes place due to vibrations in the ears. Sound waves enter the ear and move along the auditory canal until they reach the ear drum. This causes vibration.

Three small bones transmit vibrations from the ear drum to the inner ear. Information heard is sent from there to the brain where it is registered. In order for the system to work effectively, the middle ear has to be full of air. The eustachian tube is the conductor of the air and directly connects to the nose and throat. This tube must open properly for sound to be transmitted effectively.

Sometimes, children have a narrow and blocked eustachian tube which prevents it from functioning the way it should. When this happens, a vacuum forms in the middle ear; this generally leads to glue ear. The lining of the middle ear becomes inflamed and causes a glue-like substance to leak into the middle ear space which should be free for air circulation. The whole system then blocks and hearing becomes impaired.

Why do children have glue ear?

Several reasons have been suggested:

- history in the family
- bacteria after colds, flu or sore throats
- passive smoking
- cold weather
- allergies to pets, pollen or dust
- use of a dummy.

Types of glue ear

Glue ear has three levels of severity:

1. The most common type of glue ear is the least severe. Symptoms include:
   - tiredness
   - pain (earache) with or without discharge
   - withdrawal
   - distractibility
   - protest
   - clinging behaviour
   - waking at night
   - frequent colds
   - breathing through mouth
   - hearing difficulties
   - frustration
   - child appearing socially inept.

2. Chronic otitis media

   A child with this type of glue ear may have any or all of the symptoms listed above, but is likely to also have a smelly, thick discharge. There may be more significant hearing loss.

3. Acute otitis media

This most severe form of glue ear is characterised by:

- severe earache
- a high temperature
- possible discharge of blood and pus
- feeling generally unwell with sickness and/or diarrhoea
- a tendency to keep pulling their ears.

Indicators of glue ear in relation to learning

The effects of on-going bouts of glue ear have a cumulative effect on the learning process. It is unlikely that children will experience all the following indicators, but a cluster of symptoms is sufficient cause for action:

- slowness in learning
- early speech and language difficulties
- mishearing some words in speech
- reading weaknesses, particularly word recognition
- spelling difficulties: spelling not phonetically logical/omission of letters in words
- weak written language
- omission of words
- incomplete sentences
- word endings missed (particularly plurals and verb endings)
- confusion of tenses
- poor use and understanding of vocabulary
- poor general knowledge
- delay in grasp of mathematical and scientific concepts due to language limitations
- misunderstanding of instructions
- lack of understanding about rules of games in the playground or organised games
- tiredness and lethargy
- particular tiredness when listening to stories read aloud
- concentration difficulties
- easily distractible
- frustration
- child is often stressed
- feels socially isolated
- often feels insecure
- appears to be easily confused.

THE LINK TO DYSLEXIA

Some children with glue ear will go on to develop symptoms consistent with current understanding of specific learning difficulties, in particular, dyslexia. (See Chapter 3 for more detail.) In this book I have listed the signs of dyslexia typical to three age groups: pre-school, primary school and secondary school. (See Chapter 8.)

Treatment

Left untreated, acute otitis media and chronic otitis media can lead to serious complications, causing long-term damage such as deafness. Less severe glue ear – when there are no signs other than a complaint of feeling 'bunged up' – rarely causes any long-term damage, but may well affect a child's educational and social development. Further, the child might be in trouble for appearing to be unable to pay attention at school and/or at home.

Doctors will take the matter seriously. They will probably look into the child's ears with an otoscope. This measures the movement of the ear drum.

Useful information to give the doctor:

- Does the child stare at you intently when you speak? He may be trying to work out what you are saying by lip reading – this may be a sign of hearing difficulty.

- Does the child fail to notice quiet sounds to which others might be alert?

- Results of health checks at school or with the health visitor to see whether the child has reached appropriate developmental milestones.

Sometimes doctors may:

- give the condition the chance to clear up on its own
- offer antibiotic treatment
- offer decongestants
- offer nasal sprays or drops
- give ear drops
- give pain killers
- recommend the use of an 'otovent' (This is a small plastic widget with a soft balloon attached to it. The child is encouraged to blow the balloon using the nose. The idea is that it opens up the eustachian tube.)
- refer the child for a hearing test.

Hearing test

The tympanometry test (the hearing test) is a painless diagnostic test. It is designed to measure how well the middle ear is able to move and how well a child can hear. The graph the test produces – a tympanogram – will give an immediate result. If a child is over the age of four and able to co-operate, they may be referred for a full hearing test using 'pure-tone audiometry'. For younger children 'distraction' tests might be used, although these do not provide an accurate assessment of hearing loss, they are only an indicator.

Parents and teachers must be aware that diagnosis of glue ear and related difficulties in school should not be made on the basis of a one-off visit to the Ear, Nose and Throat clinic. It may be that on the day that the child attends the clinic, hearing is clearer; a week or so later it may not be. That is the nature of the condition.

SURGERY

In many cases, antibiotics and other treatments do not work sufficiently well to overcome the problem (doctors are concerned not to overdose a child on antibiotics) and so surgery may be considered. Children should not be operated on unnecessarily; anaesthesia carries its own risks and there may be a small risk of permanent perforation and occasionally, infection. However, the insertion of a small plastic tube (a grommet) is a method that is highly successful, immediate and carries a low rate of risk. As an educator, I have seen the enormous benefits of this minor operation.

To expand: doctors sometimes suggest that bilateral hearing impairment of 25–30 dB HL is sufficient to justify surgery. If the ear drum is close to bursting, an ear, nose and throat specialist might perform a myringotomy. This involves making a small hole in the ear drum under anaesthetic, so that the fluid can drain out. It is common to insert a small tube called a grommet. The purpose of the grommet is to drain the fluid, thereby allowing a free flow of air and restoring hearing. Often the child will have the adenoids removed at the same time, as these glands tend to become swollen and infected adding to the problem. There is usually an immediate result.

Figure 2 Picture of a grommet

Decisions regarding the insertion of grommets tend to be regional and happen in phases. It was a common treatment until the late 1980s, when thinking moved towards 'watchful waiting'. As a result, the number of referrals to ENT specialists dropped significantly and too many children now wait too long to have grommets inserted.

Professor Tony Wright (2004), Director of the Institute of Laryngology and Otology at the Royal Ear, Nose and Throat Hospital, London, says:

> The longer a child waits for surgery the longer these problems persist and the greater the risk of structural damage to the ear, which can lead to long-term deafness among other problems.

Professor Mark Haggard (2004), former Director of the Medical Research Council's Institute of Hearing Research believes that the correct intervention for established glue ear is surgery, particularly for those over the age of three-and-a-half, who have been clearly shown to benefit from grommets. He believes that many children do not get treatment and so have continuing problems which disadvantage them by the time they get to school.

Once the tiny tubes are inserted the child's hearing improves almost immediately. Grommets usually remain in place for several months or in some cases, years. They normally fall out themselves quite painlessly. If the problem reoccurs, discussion with a specialist will guide the parent on the viability of further surgery. Many children will have the procedure repeated if the condition is severe and continues. In some cases, the ear drum may scar and occasionally this results in mild hearing loss.

CARING FOR A CHILD WITH GROMMETS

When the child has grommets in place, it is wise not to let them put their heads in water. The use of a swimming hat is normally sufficient. When washing their hair, Vaseline on cotton wool will prevent water from entering the ear.

Eventually the grommets are expelled from the body – parents often find them on the pillow after a night's sleep. Very occasionally they have to be removed by the GP. At that point it is hoped that the condition has passed. There are cases when the tubes need to be reinserted as the glue ear has reoccurred. In that case, the process is repeated. Some children may have an allergy to milk which exacerbates the problem of glue ear. In these cases, alternatives to milk should be used until the condition clears up. Discussion with a GP or nutritionist is advisable before taking this action.

PARENTS REPORTING – POST INSERTION OF GROMMETS

As children wake up from the operating table, parents report seeing immediate and remarkable changes in their children. The children do not shout and are calmer and happier than they have been for a long time. They are pain free and as a result sleep better at night – as do the parents! At home, the television is turned down lower and children tend to play more happily with each other. The children also tend to respond better to requests as they can now hear them!

Some children have suffered the condition for so long that they need to be 're-educated' in terms of acceptable behaviour. Once a child can hear well, this process normally works quickly and effectively.

What might parents do to help?

It would be of great benefit to the child if parents and teachers were to work together, each reinforcing that which the other is doing. Good communication and sharing of information is vital to the child's well-being. Information contained in this book may be a useful starting point for better understanding of the condition and of planning ways of supporting the child.

A young child will probably seek warmth and comfort and they may be unhappy at being away from home. Parents and teachers must be aware of this and ensure that:

■ the child is comforted (and possibly medicated) when in pain; and

■ the child is given tasks that will help develop spoken language. He/she will not be able to pick up language from people around them when glue ear is stopping them from hearing clearly. These periods may continue for approximately eight weeks at a time. As a result, children may well fall behind in their early development if adults do not compensate for this.

Remember that the feelings of illness attached to hearing loss may affect a child's relationships with adults and children around them. Frequent illness may weaken their ability to interact well with others.

For the older learner, a good study skills programme should be introduced (some initial ideas are offered in this book). Where further support is necessary, parents should contact the child's teacher and/or the school's SENCo (Special Educational Needs Co-ordinator) to discuss what can be done.

Guidance for parents

If you are concerned about the medical side of the problem, speak to your health visitor or GP who can refer you to an ENT specialist if appropriate.

If you are concerned about schooling, speak to the child's teacher and the SENCo. If you feel that progress is not being made, remember that your child has rights and the school must ensure they are learning effectively.

If you feel that your child may have dyslexic tendencies, make contact with one of the organisations listed in this book – and speak to the school outlining your concerns. If the child does not make progress and the needs are severe, you may need to contact the Local Education Authority for further advice and assessment.

How parents can help a child with glue ear

1. Teach the child to listen. Gain child's attention before speaking. Turn their face towards you.

2. Do not exaggerate mouth movements. Just speak clearly.

3. Teach older children about body language and how we can pick up all sorts of non-verbal signals.

4. Remind them that it is very difficult to listen and talk at the same time. Get them to stop – listen – then speak.

5. No-one should shout at the child for losing concentration or for appearing not to follow what is going on. These children are genuinely limited in their processing of information at times.

6. The TV should be switched off when children are doing work.

7. Reduce background noise when talking to the child.

8. Make speech louder or clearer than you would normally do.

9. Get down to the child's level to talk.

10. Repeat important words – use natural intonation.

11. Turn off all background equipment which may interfere with on-going conversation.

12. Close the window if there is noise outside.

This page may be copied by the purchasing institution for use with parents

Developing language learning

1. Sing simple songs with repeated words and phrases.

2. Play word and listening games.

3. Read frequently with children, labelling and describing pictures – and let them see your lips moving.

4. Play rhyming games.

5. Engage in child's discussions and interests.

6. Play interactive games encouraging turn taking.

7. Model desired language by describing on-going activities.

8. Respond immediately and consistently to child's communication attempts.

9. Pause to give the child time to talk.

10. Give positive feedback for language attempts.

11. Elaborate on child's utterances by adding words.

12. Provide an environment rich in interesting pictures, toys and materials to provide a stimulus to encourage speaking.

© Lindsay Peer (2005) *Glue Ear*, published by David Fulton Publishers Ltd.

Games to help develop speech and language

- What word would be left if the /m/ sound were taken away from *mat*?

- Do *push* and *pull* begin with the same sound?

- What word would we have if you put these sounds together: /s/, /a/, /d/?

- What is the first sound in *toes*?

- How many sounds do you hear in the word *take*?

- What sound do you hear in *kate* that is missing in *ate*?

- What word starts with a different sound: *bat, not, brick, ball*?

- Is there a /k/ in *bike*?

© Lindsay Peer (2005) *Glue Ear*, published by David Fulton Publishers Ltd.

Education/Health professionals

1. Class teacher: this person is in the position to tell you how your child is doing, academically, socially and emotionally in the school situation. They should be able to let you know your child's strengths and weaknesses and what steps will be taken to address his/her needs.

2. SENCo (Special Educational Needs Co-ordinator): this person has the role of advisor to you and to the class teacher if there is a concern relating to any special need. They will hold a Register of Special Educational Needs and will place your child on it if sufficient progress is not made in a short space of time.

3. The head teacher: you will normally see the head teacher if you feel that there is a reason for concern which is not being adequately addressed by the class teacher and the SENCo.

4. Head of year: in a secondary school this person is responsible for the pastoral side of the child's development. They should work closely with the SENCo and be aware of the child's strengths and difficulties. This should direct their thinking and action.

This page may be copied by the purchasing institution for use with parents

5.	Teaching assistant: this person works in classrooms to assist with group work or give individual support where needed. TAs work under the direction of the SENCo and/or the class teacher.

6.	Speech and communications therapist: some children will need an assessment carried out by such a person and probably exercises to follow. These may be carried out at school and/or at home. Some children who have experienced glue ear may need this for a considerable period of time.

7.	Occupational therapist: if the child has weaknesses with poor motor co-ordination in either writing or movement, advice will be sought from this therapist. There may be need for an assessment and exercises to follow. These may be carried out at school and/or at home.

8.	Educational psychologist: this person is normally consulted when intervention by school is deemed not to be working effectively. He/she will make a full assessment of the child's strengths and weaknesses and give guidance on how best to develop their skills.

© Lindsay Peer (2005) Glue Ear, published by David Fulton Publishers Ltd.

3 How is glue ear linked to learning and dyslexia?

Episodes of glue ear can have a significant impact on a child's development and learning, particularly in areas such as speech and language, spelling and behaviour. Mild to moderate, fluctuating hearing loss means that the child receives only a partial or inconsistent auditory signal (Roberts and Wallace, 1997) and as a result, may appear distracted and disorganised. Prolonged and frequent disruptions in auditory input may obstruct sound discrimination and processing of speech. This is likely to cause the child to have incomplete or inaccurate understanding of what is being said and give them the feeling that they are 'lost' when in a busy environment. Children may experience frequent changes in intensity of sound signals, learn to tune out and develop attention difficulties – particularly when expected to listen for long periods of time. They may well be unaware that this is happening.

The hearing loss caused by glue ear (measured in decibels, dB HL) can mean that:

■ Normal speech is heard only as a whisper.

■ There is limited understanding of the spoken word in a noisy room.

■ Children cannot follow instructions or understand rules.

■ Specific sounds (phonics) cannot be used effectively when learning to read.

■ There can be difficulties when learning foreign languages.

SPEECH DEVELOPMENT

Conversational speech is not always clear and spoken at a consistent speed. Words are often run together and different people speak at varying speeds with different dialects, stresses and so on. The precision of sound production varies greatly among different speakers and even within the same speaker at different moments in time. In addition to this, environmental influences have the effect of altering perception and understanding, e.g. the distance from the speaker or the level of background noise. Hearing loss may well place an additional burden on children in the early stages of language learning. They do not have the experience to use other clues such as body language or contextual clues that would be employed by adults with hearing loss. It would seem that there are large numbers of children who experience difficulties in the development of early language and/or literacy learning who have a history of suffering glue ear to a more severe degree than most.

Some of these children find the discrimination of language and the processing of speech so problematic that they encode information incorrectly. Once language becomes so difficult that engagement is too stressful, these children will often tune out a significant amount of auditory-based information. Further the general feeling of being so unwell and of being congested over a long period may cause a problem in engaging with others in a positive way. Effects such as tiredness, withdrawal, lethargy and clinging behaviour are not unusual. Some children are also reluctant to explore the environment independently (Parmalee, 1993) and as a result have fewer opportunities to establish a knowledge base from which to experience and develop language.

Pragmatic language may also be affected as children will sometimes miss clues such as subtle nuances of language, e.g. exclamations or questions.

There are further links with poor spelling. These children find it difficult to hear low intensity sounds, e.g. /t/,/k/,/s/. If a child cannot hear the sounds, there is little chance that they will spell them. Morphological markers are also affected, as they are often spoken quietly and often end words. Thus the omission of short words in sentences or letters such as the plural 's' are often omitted from the written form.

LINKS WITH DYSLEXIA

International research (Peer, 2002) with a sample of 1,000 dyslexic young people showed that the number with a history of ear infections, specifically glue ear to be 703. This indicates that there is a sub-group of dyslexic learners, who have this early history.

This major research finding has strong implications for theory and practice. From a theoretical perspective, one intriguing possibility is that, rather than reflecting some underlying brain abnormality from birth, the difficulties in phonological processing (Snowling and Nation, 1997), in auditory magnocellular performance (Stein and Walsh, 1997) and in vestibular function (Nicolson and Fawcett, 1999) are actually acquired later in life. If a child suffers from glue ear in the early years, normal development of all of these functions simply will not take place.

A child with glue ear may experience mild to moderate fluctuating hearing loss and receive a partial or inconsistent auditory signal for considerable periods of time.

- The child may appear distracted and disorganised.

- Prolonged and frequent disruptions in auditory input may impede the development of phonological awareness and speech processing skills.

- The above causes the child to encode information incompletely and inaccurately into the 'database' from which language develops.

- Children may experience frequent changes in the intensity of auditory signals and learn to 'tune out'.

- In school, pupils may have specific difficulties with:
  - distractibility
  - working independently
  - missing spoken instructions and/or requests.

Key findings in this study show that the glue ear sub-group have dyslexic tendencies that are more severe than those found in the dyslexia group that does not suffer from glue ear. It should also be noted that whilst the majority of children worldwide experience a single bout of glue ear in their first year (Daly, 1997) only a minority go on to develop severe and continuing bouts of the condition.

Anecdotal discussions with head teachers in specialist dyslexia and other schools, teachers and parents of dyslexic children have highlighted vast numbers of children reported to have suffered from repeated ear infections; one of these reported over 90 per cent. Large numbers of these have received numerous antibiotic treatments or had grommets inserted. This corroborates the research findings above.

EARLY IDENTIFICATION

Not surprisingly, due to the impact a loss of hearing has on these children on their families and on their teachers watching reactions in school, they tend to be identified earlier than other dyslexic children.

In my research, the glue ear group of learners presented with more significant problems than other dyslexic learners when language performance was measured. In areas of both spoken language ('academic' as opposed to 'chat'), and written English, they performed at a greater deficit than the non-glue ear dyslexic group. Reading skills were also significantly poorer in that group. As a result of this, their general success across the curriculum was depressed.

There were often particular difficulties in the areas of language learning, short-term memory and behaviour. Another highly significant weakness particularly common to the glue ear group was speed of processing. This is possibly a result of intermittent and significant hearing loss for weeks or months at a time.

The causal chain for these children may look like Figure 3 opposite.

CUMULATIVE RISK FACTORS

■ It may be that some genetic abnormality predisposes 'dyslexic' children to glue ear.

■ It is almost certainly the case that the risk factors are cumulative, so that a dyslexic child who has for example, to learn more than one language and who has glue ear is particularly likely to develop literacy difficulties. This is common to both bilingual children and those attempting to learn a foreign language in school.

■ Those young children, who have suffered bouts of glue ear so severe that it has led to the insertion of grommets, have been deprived of the input that is so needed for normal development in areas of language and literacy. This loss has the effect of causing a chain of difficulties in the development of phonological awareness, ultimately leading to difficulties with reading and spelling.

■ As bouts of glue ear occur at a very young age, the early loss of consistent hearing, together with bouts of ear infections is equally likely to impact upon the vestibular system, which will affect balance and may cause ocular motor abnormalities.

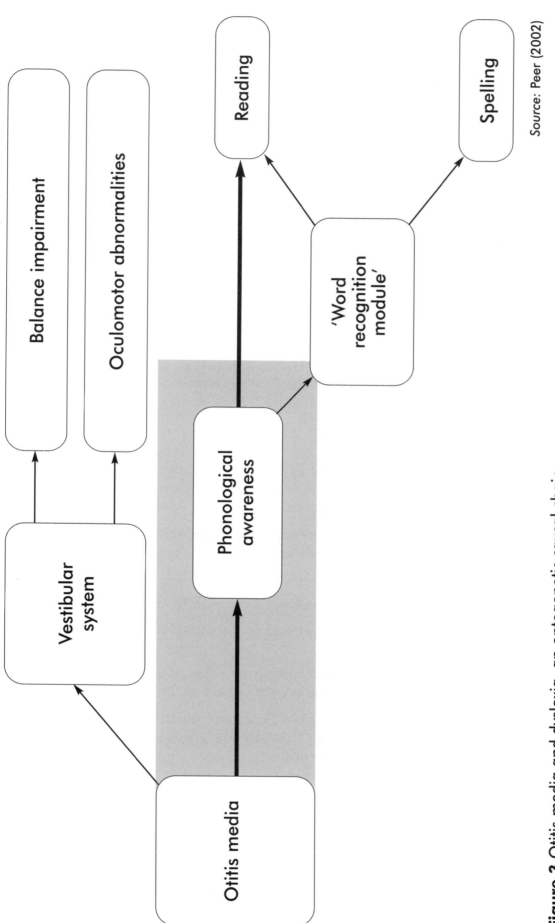

Figure 3 Otitis media and dyslexia, an ontogenetic causal chain

The research presented here opens up the possibility that a minor childhood complaint (glue ear), occurring at a time when auditory and vestibular skills are developing rapidly, may be sufficient in itself to lead to the symptoms of dyslexia.

BEHAVIOUR

Whilst not a part of the causal chain, the issue of behaviour is an important part of the story. It is quite common for children with dyslexia/glue ear to show signs of anxiety and in many cases, poor behaviour. This is often a reaction to the frustration felt by the learner when demotivation and low self-esteem set in. The results of this international study (Peer, 2002) show enhanced levels of these behaviours in the glue ear group. I would expect this when children cannot hear too well and language is spoken too fast for them to comprehend. Life perhaps seems to be passing them by and may often appear frightening. They are frequently in trouble, both at home and at school for 'not listening' and 'not concentrating', and may well be struggling in the areas of spelling, reading and writing. This too would add to the frustrations felt by learners who are so closely measured by their successes in these areas. As a result, deviant behaviours may well be documented by teachers in the classroom and/or parents at home. This is sufficient reason to assess urgently and not wait for failure to set in. Loss of self-esteem and motivation must be prevented at all costs.

THE EDUCATIONALIST'S VIEW

There are two key periods in a child's life when glue ear is highly significant – one at around two years and the other at around five years. These are critical times in a child's life in relation to language and literacy.

As the situation currently stands, early years specialists and teachers are not informed of previous hearing difficulties and the existence of glue ear:

- Parents are not asked pertinent questions.
- GPs and health visitors do not pass on the information to schools.
- Ear, Nose and Throat specialists do not explain the possible educational implications to anyone!

There seems to be no formal method for passing on relevant information from health to educational services. This must change for the benefit of the child!

Medical people must work with educationalists and with parents, appreciating that if the child continues to suffer the condition there are likely to be significant educational problem resulting from the lack of treatment.

LONG-TERM IMPACT

The consequences of glue ear can last for life. These children grow into adolescents and adults who seem to suffer from some weaknesses in at least:

- speed of processing language both spoken and written;
- following conversation when there is background noise;

- learning foreign languages;
- spelling.

Secondary school teachers need to be told how best to manage children with this history. In a busy, noisy secondary school when academic demands are very great indeed and every hour the child meets another teacher and another subject, this information is particularly important. Too many children are consistently in trouble at school for behaving in ways for which they should not be blamed. If teachers were provided with the appropriate information and acted upon it, children would react very differently. Everyone would benefit.

4 Speech and language development

The learning of spoken language is partly through interaction with others and partly biological; most people are predestined to speak. Their environment will determine which languages are spoken. The more a person verbally interacts with others, the more they are likely to develop language. The parent/carer is the first and most critical person with whom a child will interact. This interaction often dictates the future. Communication includes eye contact, facial expression and body language.

We know that babies can think before they speak and that people think in images as well as words. It is fair to assume therefore that before people learn to speak, they have a considerable amount of pre-linguistic skill in place. When language development is referred to in this section, it specifically means the production of spoken language, communication skills and the manipulation of information for cognitive and academic achievement.

Like anything else, rates of development are not consistent for all children and children learn language at different rates. What is important therefore is to be able to ascertain that the child is indeed making significant progress. When children have specific language impairments, a range of difficulties can be observed:

■ delayed onset of language;

■ difficulties in articulation in childhood;

■ on-going difficulties in understanding, producing and judging grammatical sentences.

These difficulties occur despite of the absence of cognitive problems, sensory impairment or social problems.

Children are most likely to succeed at language acquisition in their first four years of life when metabolic activity in the brain is at its peak. This is why generally a person learns languages more easily as a child and the process becomes progressively more difficult as people get older. Whilst the acquisition of vocabulary is manageable, grammar and phonology often remain problematic. Listen to an adult trying to speak a language they have just learned with the correct accent. Compare this to a child. No prizes for who tends to win!

Stages of development

Children tend to go through the same stages of language development regardless of how long it takes them. However, many children with glue ear have suffered hearing impairment at the very age that is critical for optimum language learning. As a result, their language and literacy tend not to develop as well as their peers.

STAGE 1

Initially babies are startled by loud noises and may cry as a result.

- By *six weeks*, parents can recognise different cries for fear, hunger, discomfort etc.
- By *three months*, they can recognise their mother's voice and may turn towards her.
- By *six months*, they will definitely turn towards her voice and babble a great deal.
- By *one year*, they will shout to attract attention, imitate adult sounds, understand their own name and understand 'no' and 'bye-bye'.
- *Shortly before their first birthday* some children will begin to understand and say words in isolation such as 'dolly' or 'nose'.

  However, others may not achieve this until some months later.

STAGE 2

- By *fifteen months*, they may have the beginnings of spoken vocabulary, possibly a dozen words. They will begin to experiment with sounds, using inflection in their voices and can obey simple commands such as 'Pass me teddy please.'
- By about *eighteen months* vocabulary growth increases to about two dozen words and primitive syntax begins with two-word strings, e.g. 'doggy allgone'; 'No bed'. They tend to gesture and sometimes echo the last thing that was said to them. They will begin to enjoy rhyme and begin to learn the odd word/sound in a nursery rhyme.

STAGE 3

- From *two and a half to three and a half*, language flourishes into fluent grammatical conversation. From 'Play ball. Want bottle.'. . .to. . . 'I don't want to go to bed now. I want a drink. Daddy's car needs washing. I want to help daddy.' They may have a vocabulary of 50 to 60 words and begin to use intonation implying questions. For example, 'Where mummy gone?'

Many children speak in complex sentences before they are two years old. Children suffering glue ear may well not!

STAGE 4

- At *two and a half*, children are likely to have a vocabulary of about 250 words. They are able to make connections between sounds and real objects and are developing grammatical structures. For example, they might add 'ed' to everything in the past tense 'walked', 'goned', 'taked'. They are able to use possessives – 'mummy's bag' and are beginning to understand and use comparative terms such as 'nice, nicer, nicest'.

STAGE 5

■ By *three*, children will show a significant increase in use of vocabulary. They ask endless questions, listen to stories and can carry on simple sentences.

STAGE 6

■ By *four*, speech is now intelligible. Children can give their name and address and can give an account of events that have happened. They ask meaningful questions. They are able to begin to read between the lines. They are able to learn their colours.

STAGE 7

■ By *five*, children will have a vocabulary of approximately 2,000 words. Speech is more fluent and they begin to have a love of language and its sounds.

STAGE 8

■ By *six*, a child's vocabulary will have grown to around 3,000 words. They are able to use simple grammatical tenses and are interested in the written word. They should be able to hold complex conversations. They are well aware of body language and use it appropriately.

Many children who have suffered glue ear will be way behind some of these stages for their age, especially those who suffer hearing loss during their first two years of life (Friel-Palti and Finitzo, 1990). This is likely to have an impact on the acquisition of literacy, their social and emotional development and behaviour. Although communication skills may appear normal for this group of children on entry to school, other auditory-based deficits may emerge in the classroom situation. Weaknesses are associated with:

■ listening comprehension;

■ academic achievement; and

■ attention and behavioural difficulties.

(Gravel and Wallace, 1995)

It is very important for teachers and parents to work with a speech and language communications specialist both to identify weaknesses and to provide a programme of intervention in an attempt to prevent failure at school.

5 What is dyslexia?

Dyslexia is perhaps best described as a condition that presents as a combination of strengths and weaknesses.

Facts

- Dyslexia invariably affects the writing process, particularly spelling.

- In most cases it is inherited, but sometimes it is acquired.

- People of all languages can be dyslexic. Being multilingual may exacerbate the problem, but it is not the cause.

- You may have a poor memory and be intelligent... and dyslexic!

- Sometimes dyslexia affects reading and/or the learning of maths and/or musical notation.

- Dyslexic people generally feel that they know a great deal more in their heads than they can get down on paper which causes a great deal of frustration.

- Dyslexic people often find that the speed at which others speak is often too fast for comfort.

- Sometimes dyslexic people experience movement on the page which makes reading difficult.

- You cannot become dyslexic through poor teaching.

- It cannot be cured... it is not a disease!

- It is not related to IQ.

Despite these difficulties, dyslexic people often go on to achieve to great heights. Among them are creative, talented thinkers of all descriptions – artists, scientists, engineers, architects, actors, mathematicians, entrepreneurs...

In the past, many people only discovered their own dyslexia when their children were diagnosed. Sadly many adults related tales of misfortune and failure at school. Their schools did not pick up their skills and their strengths and made no appropriate provision for them. Many children were given a rough deal in a time when little was known about the condition.

Today, much more is known about dyslexia. The growth of scientific knowledge together with advances in teaching techniques mean that each and every person has the opportunity to learn the way they learn best and ultimately fulfil their potential. Dyslexic people are certainly as able as anyone else... and in many cases, more so!

The overlap of glue ear and dyslexia

The overlap of the indicators describing dyslexia and glue ear from an educational viewpoint is considerable and highly significant. They highlight areas in the dyslexia list which it might be said are hearing-related. These are indicated by an asterisk in the list below:

- Speed of processing: spoken and written language slow.*

- Poor concentration.*

- Difficulty following instructions.*

- Forgetful of words.*

- Has poor standard of written ability compared with oral ability.

- Produces messy work with many crossings out and words tried several times, e.g. wipe, wype, wiep, wipe.

- Is persistently confused by letters which look similar, particularly b/d, p/g, p/q, n/u, m/w.

- Has poor handwriting with many reversals and badly formed letters.

- Spells a word several different ways in one piece of writing.

- Makes anagrams of words, e.g. tired for tried, breaded for bearded.*

- Produces badly set-out written work, doesn't stay close to the margin.

- Has poor pencil grip.

- Produces phonetic and/or bizarre spelling: not age/ability appropriate.*

- Uses unusual sequencing of letters or words.

- Makes poor reading progress, especially using 'Look and Say' methods.

- Finds it difficult to blend letters together.*

- Has difficulty establishing syllable division or knowing the beginnings or ends of words.*

- Pronunciation of words is unusual.*

- No expression in reading.*

- Comprehension poor.*

- Is hesitant and laboured in reading, especially when reading aloud.*

- Misses out words when reading, or adds in extra words.

- Fails to recognise familiar words.

- Loses the point of a story being read or written.*

- Has difficulty in picking out the most important points from a passage.*

- Shows confusion with number order, e.g. units, tens, hundreds.

- Is confused by symbols such as + and x signs.

- Has difficulty remembering anything in sequential order, e.g. tables, days of the week, alphabet.

- Has difficulty when learning to tell the time.
- Shows poor time keeping and general awareness.
- Has poor personal organisation.
- Has difficulty remembering what day of the week it is, their birth date, seasons of the year, months of the year.
- Difficulty with concepts – yesterday, today, tomorrow.
- Has poor motor skills, leading to weaknesses in speed, control and accuracy with the pencil.
- Has limited understanding of non-verbal communication.*
- Is confused by the difference between left and right, up and down, east and west.
- Has indeterminate hand preference.
- Performs unevenly from day to day.
- Employs work avoidance tactics, such as sharpening pencils and looking for books.
- Seems to 'dream', does not seem to listen.*
- Is easily distracted.*
- Is the class clown or is disruptive or withdrawn (these are often cries for help).*
- Is excessively tired due to amount of concentration and effort required.*

The overlap is highly significant. So what does this mean for glue ear/dyslexic leaners?

DeMarco and Givens (1989) suggest that even when children with significant and long-standing levels of glue ear have surgery and can hear better, there may well be continuing weaknesses that could not be predicted. In a case study, they showed that whilst some weaknesses in hearing were indeed overcome when sounds were heard at a louder level, some of the speech discrimination issues still remained.

THE NEED FOR ASSESSMENT

These findings clearly indicate the need for appropriate assessment and support. Currently there is little or no recognition of the need for provision for children with this specific area of weakness, which is so very critical to the learning process.

Screening should take place to identify children at risk of difficulties with speech and language noting that they may be linked to academic and behavioural weaknesses. For children going into primary school, it may be necessary to screen on a regular basis, ensuring that teachers and parents are made aware of the fluctuating levels of difficulty that the child may be experiencing. Supporting the child through the learning process, when the ability to hear or work effectively is impaired will be of great value to achievement and ultimately to self-esteem.

6 Spotting the signs of overlapping conditions and taking appropriate action

Differing levels of hearing loss will have an impact on a child's learning and behaviour and affect their interactions with, and responsiveness to, their environment. Frequent illness may weaken their ability to interact well with others. Glue ear may cause tiredness, pain, withdrawal, lethargy, making a child easily distracted, and clingy. In the young child, it is likely that warmth and comfort will be sought and they will be less happy at being away from home than would be hoped. Parents and teachers must be aware of this and ensure that the child is comforted (and possibly medicated) when in pain and is given tasks that will help develop spoken language. Children suffering differing levels of hearing loss will not be able to pick up language from the environment around them at certain times – often up to eight weeks at a time after a common cold. As a result, they may well fall behind in their early development. Adults should help compensate for this.

Teachers and parents must be aware that prolonged or frequent episodes of glue ear may limit child development in:

- attention (they may be easily distracted);

- speech and language (vocabulary, grammatical structures and flow of language);

- independent working (if they are unaware of specific tasks and of explanation going on around them); and

- academic achievement.

Many health professionals and teachers are yet to appreciate the impact of frequent bouts of glue ear. Information must be passed on to schools and implications made clear to parents. Parents and teachers must ensure that the home and the classroom are set up in such a way that the children can function, despite their difficulties. They should ensure that no-one shouts at the child for losing concentration or for appearing not to follow what is going on in any particular environment. These children are, at times, genuinely limited in their processing of information.

Spotting the signs of overlapping conditions

It is well known that there is a significant overlap for some children who experience dyslexia and have, or have had, speech and language difficulties. That being the case, teachers should look out for any obvious speech difficulties, unexpectedly poor educational progress or the emergence of behavioural difficulties. They will be aware of weak comprehension and/or poor phonological processing skills in the learners in their class. These children find it very difficult to learn 'automatically' and to retain the information taught. One of the best ways is to 'over-teach', leading to 'over-learning' which is necessary to ensure that specific knowledge is remembered, internalised and enters free speech.

Self-esteem in these children is often quite low as a result of on-going pain, the constant struggle to concentrate and specific difficulties in learning. Consequently, those living and working with them need to plan ways to develop self-esteem. For those children who find spoken communication problematic, useful comments might be something like:

> *I am sorry I didn't understand what you just said. Why don't you try again? Your speech is getting better as the weeks go by. Well done for working so hard at it.*

Sometimes dyslexic children have problems with expressive language – finding the right words to express what they mean. Sometimes they may use the wrong words altogether: 'What a pretty flutterby.' and 'My mummy is dying from a brain tuna.' were two comments made to me.

Children who additionally have a glue ear background to their specific learning difficulty profiles often experience receptive language weakness as they lose so much of what is going on around them. Speed of processing is often much slower than would be anticipated in these children; surprisingly this may also appear in the understanding of the written as well as in the spoken word. Difficulty answering questions and not following instructions are sometimes the first clues that teachers have when working with these children.

In older children, teachers should watch out for the child who develops strategies for buying time and avoids eye contact. They might also find excuses for leaving the room when it is about to be their turn to do something in front of others – such as read aloud – when they know they can't do it well enough. They are protecting themselves from humiliation.

When trying to identify young children with a range of speech and communication difficulties in addition to dyslexia, teachers should look out for the child who:

- Confuses vowels and consonants.
- Finds difficulty learning phonics.
- Finds imitation of simple clapping rhythms difficult.
- Can't sing songs or nursery rhymes as others do.
- Has poor concentration.
- Is easily distractible.
- Has difficulty in understanding sequencing language and activities, e.g. before, after.
- Has difficulty learning order of days of week, months, times tables.
- Can't hold much information in memory.

- Omits beginnings and endings of words, e.g. 'pretending' becomes 'tending'.
- Reduces multi-syllabic words, e.g. 'potato' becomes 'tato'.
- Speaks unclearly when excited.
- Speaks unclearly when attempting a lengthy sentence.
- Shows persistent confusion between voiced and unvoiced sounds, e.g. p/b, t/d, k/g or word confusion such as zink/think, bed/bet, ink/ing.
- Has delayed understanding of question words, e.g. Who? What?
- Finds following instructions without prompting problematic.
- Offers limited verbal comments on activities of self or of others.
- Gives unexpected responses to questions.
- Has difficulty following a story without many visual clues.
- Has little play involving sounds, rhymes or words.
- Enjoys the visual content of TV, but finds it hard to follow the plot and story.
- Has difficulty with words relating to time, e.g. tea time, end of break, evening.
- Has difficulty with prepositions and adverbs.
- Has literal interpretation of idioms, e.g. 'Pull your socks up!' ('Dad's tied up at the office' caused one of my students great consternation!)
- Confuses grammar, e.g. 'Where book?'

These children will find the everyday learning, playing and social development in a classroom problematic. Teachers and their assistants should ensure that needs are understood and that appropriate intervention is put in place as soon as they are identified.

VISUAL DIFFICULTIES

When reading, some children find tracking difficult. They may repeat a line, read the one above again or perhaps the one below. This complicates the task of comprehending what they have just read. When taken to an optician, some of these children have been found to have excellent eyesight, but unexpectedly still have visual problems with the written word. Their visual difficulties compound their learning difficulties. Many behavioural optometrists are now identifying such problems and offering solutions. They might include:

- eye exercises;
- coloured lenses or plastic sheets;
- making the page larger;
- a larger font;
- suggesting that the learner works on paper which is off-white.

For children who answer yes to any of the following, it is worth having their eyes checked out by a specialist in the field:

- Do they see blurring?

- Do the letters and/or the words move on the paper?
- Do they have to work hard to focus on reading?
- Do they fail to understand what they have read and/or do they often have to re-read for information?
- Do they prefer to read on pastel coloured paper?
- Do they prefer to read magazines or newspapers (with narrow columns) rather than books (with a wide sweep)?
- Do they dislike bright lights?
- Are their eyes sometimes sore or do they water?
- Do they feel sick when reading in a car?

THE PLAYGROUND

The playground can be quite a frightening place for children with glue ear in a number of ways. Sometimes, the children are prime targets of bullying – sometimes verbal and other times physical. Experience tells me that those children who are either speech and language delayed or who are dyspraxic, are often the ones who are most vulnerable.

Other frustrations include missing out on conversations among friends or even not playing with other children as they haven't heard what is happening or understood what to do. As a result of feeling ostracised, children sometimes show behavioural problems which need to be understood and dealt with. Is the child's poor behaviour due to frustration, bullying etc. or is it something else? The response from the school should match the underlying cause.

Helpful activities

DEVELOPING RHYTHM AND RHYME

- Clapping around a circle.
- Tapping out children's names – or other vocabulary.
- Leader claps a tune and children copy.
- Singing of nursery rhymes or songs. (Allow the child who cannot follow to sit opposite the leader and look intently at their lips. They will hopefully then be in a better position to follow.)
- Use rhyming picture cards.
- Rhyming 'I spy'.

VOCABULARY

- Use multisensory approaches to develop language.
- For younger ones: use objects and pictures.

- For older ones: use antonyms, synonyms, root words, categorisations, associations, multiple meanings.
- Use newspapers, comics and magazines.
- Word associations.
- Pairs.
- Twenty questions.
- Oral games.

GRAMMAR

- Positional prepositions – teach place: in, on, under etc.

  Note the child who disappeared out of the classroom when his teacher said to him 'You can go out when you have tidied your desk.' He was out before she had a chance to finish! He heard, 'Go out . . . tidy'. The teacher may have had more success had she said 'Tidy your desk then you can go out.' He would have heard 'Tidy – go out'. Sequence and order are important.

  Reinforce the use of prepositions across the curriculum, e.g. in the classroom and playground for young children and in subject areas for older ones.

PLURALS

These may be missed in reading, spelling or speaking.

- Use games: miming, number rhymes.
- Use colour to show where and how they should be added.
- Hold a little mirror next to the mouth to show the child the movement of the lips, tongue and teeth. This helps (*MTSR programme*).

TENSES

Predictions and retelling work in reading activities are useful ways of reinforcing knowledge of tenses.

Relating children's activities to their lives are helpful too. For example asking them to tell what they did over the weekend, what they will be doing next week, on holiday etc. What happened in the news, in a film they saw or in a book they read?

Passive structures are particularly difficult. This needs to be taught early and well used over the years. Public examination papers still use them in questions. If the tense has not been understood, children may well fail a paper because they did not understand the question, not because they did not know the answer to it!

OMISSIONS

These children often miss out the little words: a, as, and, the, plural 's'. Teach older learners to check for these as part of their proof-reading process. Use coloured highlighter pens in newspaper passages to identify key words and phrases and ensure that the small words are not omitted in the reading and writing process.

Difficulty learning rules of language

SOUNDS (PHONOLOGY)

Hearing loss will mean that certain sounds may not be heard at all or if they are, they will be very unclear. For example, t, k, s, sh. Unstressed syllables, e.g. ba in 'banana' may be lost as well as final consonants, e.g. t as in 'hat'. If that happens you may see it in the way the child spells a word or in their speech.

MEANINGS (SEMANTICS)

Children who have suffered extensive bouts of glue ear, may find that their perception of morphologic markers (the smallest unit of meaning), e.g. –s, to mark plurality or possession is missing, as they do not hear the sounds. These will have to be taught. Short words, e.g. 'is', 'the' that are spoken rapidly and softly are often lost too.

GRAMMAR (SYNTAX)

The children may misperceive words and as a result, remember them less successfully. In some extreme cases, grammar may need to be taught in a way which is more suited to those learning English as a foreign language as they will need to learn the rules rather than acquire grammar instinctively.

USES (PRAGMATICS)

As the ability to follow conversation may be limited, some of these learners may miss subtle nuances of language, e.g. intonation, questions. If they seem not to answer the question or to go off track, it may be that this is the cause of the difficulty.

MEMORY

(a) Word finding

- Try prompting by giving the first sound in the word or with a description of size, colour etc.
- Give opposite clues – 'It's not black, its…(white).'
- Give similar clues – 'It's like a mouse, it's a…(rat).'

(b) Short-term auditory memory

- Listen to stories on tape, then answer questions.
- Chunk language and get them to repeat what you have said. As these children find remembering instructions problematic, start with one, then build up to several.

- Build memory tasks into curriculum lessons and ensure that the child is not asked to do more than they can comfortably handle, e.g. in music – how to play; in geography – how to follow directions; in maths – how to work with calculators.

All the aspects listed may affect later academic achievement, particularly in reading, writing and language-based subjects.

ORGANISATION

Many of these children are disorganised. Teachers and parents should work together to develop skills in this area. They need to learn to take care of their own belongings and to organise their work at home and at school. For some, this is a real challenge. Ask their parents!

Try some of the following:

- Take responsibility for something in class.
- Take message(s) for the teacher.
- Teach the children how to organise their desk or locker.
- For older learners, make effective use of a Filofax, electronic notebook etc.
- Ensure materials ready for school and homework. Ask for the support of parents.

FURTHER ACTIVITIES

- Look at letters, finger trace on rough and smooth surfaces.
- Link letter names with their sounds.
- Link speech articulation with spelling.
- Use phonological awareness tasks.
- Count the syllables in words.
- Count the letters and sounds in words.
- Separate out and bring together sounds, e.g. 'c-a-t' says 'cat'.
- And, conversely, 'cat' says 'c-a-t'.

SPEAKING, LISTENING AND UNDERSTANDING

For some children who are really struggling there might be a need to simplify language. By making sentences less complex, the ideas will be more easily understood. Simplify and rephrase language if necessary and take out unnecessary words. There may be a need to explain specific items of vocabulary; visual clues will help if possible and if appropriate. A useful technique is to ask the pupil to repeat back, in their own words, what has been said or what the task ahead might be. 'Chunking' language is a good way to ensure that each piece is understood and held in memory. Adding a pause to process what has been said, will aid long-term internalisation. Together with extra time for processing the language, the child's weaknesses will not prevent participation and development.

Sometimes, with older children in particular, they have experienced such 'traumas' in the classroom that they are very hesitant to perform verbally in front of others. One way might be to make a private arrangement with them (Lavoie, 1990). It works in the following way. You tell the learner that if you are standing in front of them, it means that you are about to ask them a question. If you have moved elsewhere, they can attend without fear of questioning. When you do ask a question, ensure that it is something that you know they can succeed in answering; give them some time to process the question and give the answer. You might decide to turn and erase the board then to buy them time. The gift of time is the greatest gift you can give any of these learners. What you will expect to see is that they answer successfully, feel pleased and then start to put up their hand so that you will ask them. This means that they will:

- value you more;
- begin to feel more confident;
- build self-esteem in your subject;
- begin to enjoy your subject more than they did. They are then likely to achieve higher grades.

Check that they understand what they are reading. Many children are able to read quite well but when asked what they have read, they have little understanding. Those listening to them reading, should be aware of this and work with them to develop this skill.

ADDITIONAL TECHNIQUES

- Use structured, sequential, multisensory spelling programmes. These will reinforce the sound–letter connections in a way that will help bypass some of their difficulties.
- Use IT to support teaching.
- Allow them to have short breaks to relax.
- Give relaxation exercises to do at an appropriate time if necessary.

MODERN FOREIGN LANGUAGES

Children learning second or subsequent languages who have or have had a difficulty with glue ear and/or dyslexia will often find themselves significantly challenged. This may be both when attempting to acquire a foreign language and when living in a multilingual setting (Peer and Reid, 2000). Some languages are more 'transparent' than others. They are easier to read and write as there is a direct connection between the letters and the sounds. Other languages, such as English, are more 'opaque'. In English, we often do not read or write words in the way they sound at all! Take for example: 'cough', 'bough', 'thought' and 'though'! Time for listening and processing has to be even longer than when learning their first language. Some languages are even more complicated as they have sounds that do not exist in the child's mother tongue – for example the guttural sounds in Arabic and in German.

Traditionally many, but not all, glue ear/dyslexic children have struggled with learning languages at school. It is not easy for some children to be given lists of words to remember and spell in another language when they are struggling in their first language! Often the children cannot 'hear' the specific sounds that they are expected to acquire and struggle to keep up with the teacher speaking at speed in a foreign tongue. Teachers must slow down.

Moreover, if children are asked to listen to native speakers on tape, this may be impossible for them. If their own teacher says the words slowly in an accent to which they are accustomed, they will do much better.

If these children are taught another language, it might be helpful to teach Italian or Spanish rather than French, for the reasons outlined above. Further, languages should be presented in a multisensory way, so that there is a greater chance of acquisition (Schneider, 1999; Schneider et al., 1999).

GROSS AND FINE MOTOR SKILL DEVELOPMENT

Some children find controlling their hand movements more difficult than others. For them, regular exercises, involving their whole body, or just moving their fingers are very useful.

A handwriting system which is joined and clear and is introduced at the beginning of school is best for these children. It helps the flow and may help prevent reversals in some children who may write their letters backwards.

Pencil grips are often used in primary school. However, in secondary school these might be replaced by triangular pens or pencils which do not look 'special'. The use of a sloping desk top is invaluable for some children as they find that it gives them more control over their writing hand.

Documented and structured support in school

■ There should be clear liaison between teachers, learning support assistants, parent, school, SENCos and the speech and communications therapist. At all points the child should be involved and know that their personal contribution is critical to achievement. The message should be that the work is not being done *to* or *for* the child, but *with* the child. That way, more effective and swifter progress is likely to be made.

A programme should be implemented which takes into consideration the general learning needs of the child within a whole class situation and also offers provision for extra support should it be deemed necessary.

■ Group and individual education plans should be prepared which reflect how and when the child will receive support.
  – The group plan is for the benefit of a number of children who need support in relation to certain aspects of the learning process.
  – The individual plan should be for the areas of need which are specific to that child.

It is critical that all the objectives are listed, that they are clear for all to understand and are acted upon.

- All targets should be small, measurable and progressive. The child particularly needs to see that progress is being made.

- All teachers and teaching assistants across the curriculum need to understand the issues and be told how best to work with the child. Gains will be little and slow if the only intervention is through one or two sessions a week; they must be reinforced by all staff in all classes at all times. Most of the class recommendations are useful to all children so this should not be an extra burden for the teacher.

- The teaching assistant must be taught by specialists how to best support the child in all circumstances should this be necessary.

- Awareness throughout the school should be made through initial notification and then regular meetings where information is disseminated and ideas are shared.

- Ensure annual reviews and IEP meetings take place and that parents are both invited and contribute. Listen to the child's perception of what works and what does not. Their contribution is often most profound.

7 Reading, glue ear and dyslexia

Learning to read

First we learn to speak; this is a biological behaviour which most children learn to do to quite a level of sophistication. However, reading is not developmental or natural; it is a learned skill.

It is thought that there are several factors that need to be in place for us to become effective readers:

- phonological awareness
- letter–word correspondence skills
- knowledge of an alphabet
- exposure to print
- morphological awareness
- fluent word recognition
- comprehension skills.

A number of children and adults with specific learning difficulties sometimes have a persistent deficit in this skill, rather than a developmental lag. If children fall behind at an early age and do not receive appropriate intervention, they will fall further and further behind.

Some dyslexic children read quite well; others read poorly or not at all. Some when reading add in extra words, others omit some. Some read fairly well, but when asked what they have read, have little idea, so have to re-read.

By the time children are part way through primary school there is an expectation that they can understand text, interpret that which they have read, relate the text to their own background and take a view on the subject. Further they will be exposed to vocabulary which is beyond that which they use and with which they are familiar. As they progress through school they will meet technical and subject-specific language which will place greater demands on their academic efforts.

It has to be said that the English language is more difficult than many others as it has a very difficult spelling system; the vowels in particular are most complex. However, people learning to read and write in all languages may have dyslexic-type difficulties.

Stages of literacy development

■ Stage 1: Long before reading and writing (Preliterate)

- ■ Speech and language develop
- ■ Communication develops
- ■ Symbols are beginning to be understood

■ Stage 2: Early interest in literacy (Logographic)

- ■ Interest in print
- ■ Pretend reading
- ■ Pretend writing

■ Stage 3: Beginning to understand written word (Alphabetic)

- ■ Auditory discrimination
- ■ Auditory memory
- ■ Auditory sequencing
- ■ Phonological representation
- ■ Phonological awareness
- ■ Articulatory skills
- ■ Alphabetic knowledge
- ■ Orthographic knowledge
- ■ Visual memory

■ Stage 4: Reading and writing (Orthographic)

Stages 1–3 plus

- ■ Morphological awareness
- ■ Orthographic representations

Source: Based on the skills outlined as essential for becoming literate by Frith (1996).

Phonological awareness

Over the past forty years, much evidence has been gathered which shows that there is a direct link between children's ability to learn to read and the ability to manipulate sounds in words. It has therefore been thought that if children are given phonological skills training, it might help prevent them from experiencing undue difficulty learning to read.

> It is important to note that in relation to children struggling with literacy who also have a history of bouts of glue ear, it is never really known when they can hear sufficiently clearly to differentiate between specific sounds and follow what is being said to them. This will substantially complicate any programme which relies on the discernment of sounds. Such children may suffer for up to eight weeks after a common cold before they can function as well as their peers.

Research has shown that phonological training alone is not sufficient to overcome any potential difficulties. It has to be delivered in combination with the teaching of a broader literacy skills programme. Visual teaching methods are also insufficient for many children on their own (Adams, 1990).

We must recognise, however, the very real challenges facing children with glue ear, even when they receive high quality specialist teaching.

Phonemic awareness

A lack of phonemic awareness is a major obstacle to learning to read. This is likely to lead to a difficulty turning spelling into sounds (Stanovich and Siegel, 1994). If a child has a problem with fluctuating hearing loss, this will directly affect their ability to learn to read fluently, comprehend at speed and spell correctly.

TEACHING OF PHONEMIC AWARENESS

Research (Cunningham, 1990) suggests that teaching the following phonemic awareness tasks has a positive effect on acquisition of reading and spelling for non-readers. Areas to note are particularly:

- rhyming, e.g. mat, cat, fat;
- auditorily discriminating sounds that are different, e.g. zinc, think;
- blending spoken sounds into words, e.g. e-le-ph-ant;
- deleting sounds from words, e.g. meat … eat.

All of these tasks are directly related to the need for clear 'hearing'.

EXAMPLES OF PHONEMIC AWARENESS TASKS FOR HOME AND SCHOOL

- *Phoneme deletion:* What word would be left if the /k/ sound were taken away from *cat*?

- *Word to word matching*: Do *pen* and *pipe* begin with the same sound?

- *Blending*: What word would we have if you put those sounds together: /s/, /a/, /t/?

- *Sound isolation*: What is the first sound in *rose*?

- *Phoneme segmentation*: How many sounds do you hear in the word *cake*?

- *Deleting phonemes*: What sound do you hear in *meat* that is missing in *eat*?

- *Odd word out*: What word starts with a different sound: *bag, nine, beach, bike*?

- *Sound to word matching*: Is there a /k/ in *bike*?

(Stanovich, 1994)

TEACHING SOUND–SPELLING CORRESPONDENCES EXPLICITLY

It is important that children are aware of the sounds of letters alongside their written representation.

Playing games whereby the phonemes are isolated is very helpful. For example, the educator holds a card with the letter 'm' on it and says: 'This is mmmm.' The children then look at the card and say the sound out loud. Ensure that the child is facing you, as they are likely to be reading your lips until they have grasped the sound. Link the sound into words they know, e.g. 'm' is for 'mummy'. Let them offer you words they can think of, e.g. mouse, monkey, medicine. Each day, the child should revise phonemes already learned and then learn one new one using such a method. Five to ten minutes per day for young children on this task is sufficient for review and acquisition. Do not be tempted to remove those cards that they have learned. Over-learning is essential for 'good remembering' for these children. When beginning to read, it is essential that children are only given 'meaningful stories' that include just the letters/sounds that they have learned. If the child is taught according to the order of the alphabet, i.e. a,b,c, there is very little they will be able to read other than the word 'cab'. If for example, they are taught p,a,t, as the first three sound–spelling relationships, they will be able to read 'Pat, tap, apt'. The context, familiarity and over-learning will all help reinforce retention.

Phonemic awareness training is not enough for many children. Foorman *et al.* (1991) showed that children also need explicit, systematic instruction in sound–spelling correspondences too. They discovered that 45 minutes of intensive sound–spelling instruction per day during reading was more effective than teaching word parts and transferring them to other words.

MORPHOLOGICAL AWARENESS

Children initially need to master the early stages of reading:

- Phonological awareness which includes rhyming with pictures and spoken words; segmenting sounds; manipulating and blending sounds.

- The alphabet including letter names and sounds; consonants and vowels.

- Syllables and their rules.

Once they have grasped this, it is invaluable to teach them morphological awareness, as from mid-primary school onwards they will be faced with many words that are morphologically complex (Nagey *et al.*, 1989). Morphology refers to the smallest meaningful unit of language. For example, an 's' at the end of the words will signify that it is a plural; an apostrophe will signify that the item belongs to someone. Teaching the meaning of prefixes and suffixes and making links to a range of words will help the children transfer meaning across the curriculum. For example,

- 'sub' meaning 'under/from below' will be helpful in understanding 'subway', 'subtract', 'subordinate', 'subversive';
- 'mis' meaning 'error' will help understanding 'mistake'; 'mislead', 'mismanage', 'misprint';
- 'ad' (ac-, af-, ag-, al-, ap-, ar-, as-, at-) means 'to' or 'toward'. For example, address, allot, affix, assign.

Likewise, in grammar, suffixes such as:

- 'ing' will tell us that something is/was happening;
- 'ed' will tell us that it happened in the past, e.g. learned, grounded, sounded.

At a later stage, morphemic awareness can help us break down words into separate pieces of meaning, such as:

- 'shipyard', 'dockland', 'notebook', 'football'.

Teachers can then go into the spelling rules that link with these.

- For example, a word drops an 'e' when adding a vowel suffix, e.g. hope . . . hoping; save . . . saving.

Some children respond well to knowing the root of the language from whence words were derived. For example, have words come from Latin, Greek or Anglo Saxon? Children who respond well to roots and logic may benefit from knowledge of this.

- For example, Greek words appear a great deal in science books. A child will find reading of the word 'chlorophyll' much easier if they know that in Greek the /ch/ sound is mostly pronounced /k/.

Whatever you teach, the use of multisensory techniques will be helpful. The more ways you find to input to the child's thinking, the greater the likelihood that it will be remembered.

TEACHING IN A STRUCTURED, SEQUENTIAL AND MULTISENSORY WAY

Multisensory teaching encourages young children to use their whole bodies, as well as their voices in the learning of letters too. Whilst speaking out loud they might:

- write in the air using large movements;
- write in a sand tray;
- curl into the shapes of letters on the floor;
- draw on a white board using different coloured pens;
- use plasticine/play dough to recreate the letters;
- use a keyboard to find specific letters then colour them.

All these techniques are fun for little ones and help reinforce the letters and sounds they need to learn.

Once a good number of letters and sounds have been learned, children can be given short texts where they are required to decode most of them, perhaps 80 per cent and go on to predict much of the rest from the context.

Children need to be taught how to 'sound out' the words. They need to know which direction they need to go in order to read them out – in English, left to right. This is sometimes forgotten, so teachers and parents need to remind them often if they are unsure. Never take anything for granted!

Clearly at the beginning of the process, the text will be simple. As they learn more letters and sounds, texts will increase in complexity. Remember that even though children might have problems with the acquisition of reading and/or spelling, they are intellectually as able as any other child. Aim high and they will respond!

Struggling older readers

For older children experiencing problems, a course such as those suggested above using playing cards and worksheets, will give them the opportunity of reviewing letters and their sounds in a structured, sequential multisensory way.

- **Over-learning** is critical if they are to overcome their weaknesses. It is very important that children are given materials to read that are in subject areas that interest them.

- **Motivation** is a key factor in attempting a task which is highly challenging.

- **Frequency** of practice is vital – just like great sports people. Daily practice is needed for success.

Like anything else, if it is not practiced, accomplishment will not be achieved. It is vital to remember however, that children should be taught in a structured and sequential way so that success, not failure, is reinforced.

In order for children to derive meaning from print they must become skilled in the Six Dimensions of Reading (Office of Elementary and Secondary Education's *Reading Excellence Act*, 2002: USA) These are:

- The skills and knowledge to understand how phonemes, or speech sounds, are connected to print.

- The ability to decode unfamiliar words.

- The ability to read fluently.

- Sufficient background information and vocabulary to foster reading comprehension.

- The development of appropriate active strategies to construct meaning from print.

- The development and maintenance of a motivation to read.

Children who are still struggling when they reach upper primary and secondary school find it increasingly more difficult to catch up. They are embarrassed to read out loud and find the whole process of learning challenging. If they could 'say' everything aloud, they would probably do well. The very fact that they have to read and write causes major difficulties for them.

Research suggests that the more one reads, the more one acquires essential language, cognitive skills and the background knowledge that promotes academic success (Cunningham and Stanovich, 1998). Reading helps to extend vocabulary, new concepts and new ways of thinking. For those who do not experience difficulties in reading, practice eventually makes the whole process automatic and ultimately, a pleasurable experience.

Conversely, those people who do not read well tend not to want to read. If they do not understand what they read, there is no pleasure in doing so. For them, the task becomes tedious and unsatisfactory. Ultimately, the gap widens between them and their peers and they fall further and further behind.

COMPREHENSION

Reading is not only about the laborious sounding out of words. It is ultimately about comprehension – which is tied in with background knowledge, vocabulary and decoding skills. If the texts presented to these children are too difficult for them, they will not read them, as very little makes sense.

It is very important that teachers and parents read stories to their children often so that the children acquire the joy of literature, even if they cannot read initially themselves. Teachers might give activities to the class based on what they have heard; they should always remember to face the child with glue ear, so that they can read the teacher's lips. This will also help to build oral skills, which are critical for children with glue ear difficulties.

All children have better oral comprehension than they do reading comprehension. All texts heard by them should be at their oral level of understanding, not at their productive reading level if we wish to stretch them and develop their intellectual capacity. Initially when older children start to read alone, they should be given books that are simple and literal.

When presented with texts to read with an adult, comprehension strategies and new vocabulary should be presented orally, with as many visual clues as possible. Teachers and parents should discuss the meaning of text with children to help enhance greater understanding. It is hoped that the strategies that teachers demonstrate and use with children, they themselves will then internalise and use at a later date.

STRUCTURED PROGRAMMES

There are many programmes that are available on the market which can be used to teach children who have areas of weakness related to the perception of sounds. Programmes such as 'Alpha to Omega' (Hornsby International Centre), 'Units of Sound' programme (Dyslexia Institute) and A Multisensory Teaching System for

Reading (Manchester Metropolitan University) are such examples. 'Touch, Type, Read and Spell' uses the same theory and employs the use of a computer which older learners in particular may prefer.

There are programmes that parents might find useful at home. Schools might wish to discuss them with the parents to ensure that the methods used are appropriate.

Older children often find the use of taped stories useful. For children who find reading challenging due to dyslexia or similar difficulties, they can become members of the charity 'Listening Books' or their local library and take out taped books on a regular basis.

Other children who are reluctant readers, but are ready for the challenge might look at books such as those in the series published by Barrington Stoke. These books are for children and adults and offer high intellectual material whilst written at a low literacy level. Interestingly, the editors of these books themselves are dyslexic and others are reluctant readers. It is their input which makes these books so acceptable to others like them.

Our aim is for children to become fluent readers. Fluency is described as '..the ability to read connected text rapidly, smoothly, effortlessly and automatically with little conscious attention to the mechanics of reading such as decoding' (Meyer and Felton, 1999).

When pupils are struggling at the decoding level, there is no space left for comprehension. It would appear that 'repeated reading' is one way to help children become more fluent readers.

FINALLY . . .

It is clear that children need to have their needs identified early and that schools should intervene as soon as there are signs that a child is falling behind. No child should be left to flounder. Action should be swift and appropriate; watchful waiting is a waste of a child's precious learning time. The limitations caused by dyslexia, glue ear and similar conditions are not the fault of the child or their parents. Much can be done to effect change and prevent the downward spiral into failure. The longer the child is left behind, the lower the self-esteem and ultimately, motivation. Too many of these children are eventually labelled Special Educational Needs (SEN) when in fact, they need not reach that level. If appropriate intervention took place as soon as a particular condition was recognised, they would be likely to do much better both academically and emotionally.

8 Specific indicators of dyslexia

Pre-school children

There is a large body of research linking speech and language difficulties in early childhood to later literacy problems. As much as possible should be done pre-school to help a child at risk. Therefore, early identification is really important. If children suffer from hearing difficulties, earache or glue ear over a significant period of time, the likelihood is that they will have a slow start to speech and communication and may have later problems with the acquisition of the written word.

Although some children may have difficulties with some parts of their learning, they may be just as bright and able as their peers – in some cases even brighter! They are often creative and imaginative. At the same time they also have difficulties. If a child shows a cluster of difficulties, you will need to take action.

SOME IDENTIFIERS

The child:

- has difficulty learning nursery rhymes;
- finds difficulty paying attention, sitting still, listening to stories;
- likes listening to stories but shows no interest in letters or words;
- seems not to follow instructions;
- has difficulty learning to sing or recite the alphabet;
- has a history of slow speech development;
- gets words muddled, e.g. cubumber, flutterby;
- has difficulty keeping simple rhythm;
- finds it hard to carry out two or more instructions at one time (e.g. put the toys in the box, then put the box on the shelf) but is fine if tasks are presented in smaller units;
- forgets names of friends, teacher, colours;
- has poor auditory discrimination;
- finds difficulty cutting, sticking and crayoning in comparison with their peer group;
- has persistent difficulty in dressing, e.g. finds shoelaces and buttons difficult;
- puts clothes on the wrong way round;

- has difficulty with catching, kicking or throwing a ball;
- often trips, bumps into things and falls over;
- has difficulty hopping or skipping;
- has obvious 'good' and 'bad' days for no apparent reason.

A child who has a cluster of these difficulties, together with some abilities may be dyslexic, but remember that the levels of development and speed of learning at the pre-school stage will differ significantly for each child.

If you are concerned about a child, consult with the special needs advisor. There are programmes and games to help with development in speech and language, motor skills, auditory and visual perception and memory. If there are problems due to glue ear, a doctor should see the child; they may refer on for hearing tests. This should give vital information to both parents and teachers.

Children in primary school

GENERAL

- speed of processing: spoken and/or written language slow;
- poor concentration;
- difficulty following instructions;
- forgetful of words;
- difficulty remembering anything in a sequential order, e.g. tables, days of the week, the alphabet.

WRITTEN WORK

The child:

- has a poor standard of written work compared with oral ability;
- produces messy work with many crossings out;
- is persistently confused by letters which look similar, particularly b/d, p/g, p/q, n/u, m/w;
- has poor handwriting, possibly with 'reversals' and badly formed letters;
- spells a word several different ways in one piece of writing, e.g. wippe, wype, wiep, wipe;
- makes anagrams of words, e.g. tired for tried, breaded for bearded;
- produces badly set-out written work, doesn't stay close to the margin;
- has poor pencil grip;
- produces phonetic and bizarre spelling: not age/ability appropriate;
- uses unusual sequencing of letters or words.

READING

The child:

- makes poor reading progress;

- finds it difficult to blend letters together;

- has difficulty in establishing syllable division or knowing the beginnings and endings of words;

- has no expression in reading;

- has a poor approach to comprehension;

- is hesitant and laboured in reading, especially when reading aloud;

- misses out words when reading, or adds extra words;

- fails to recognise familiar words;

- loses the point of a story being read or written;

- has difficulty in picking out the most important points from a passage.

NUMERACY

The child:

- shows confusion with number order, e.g. units, tens, hundreds;

- is confused by symbols such as + and x signs;

- has difficulty remembering anything in a sequential order, e.g. tables, days of the week, the alphabet;

- has difficulty learning and remembering times tables;

- may reverse numbers 2 . . . 5.

TIME

The child:

- has difficulty in learning to tell the time;

- shows poor time keeping and general awareness;

- has poor personal organisation;

- has difficulty remembering what day of the week it is: birth date, seasons of the year, months of the year;

- has difficulty with concepts – yesterday, today, tomorrow.

SKILLS

The child:

- has poor motor skills, leading to weaknesses in speed, control and accuracy of the pencil;

- has a limited understanding of non-verbal communication;
- is confused by the difference between left and right, up and down, east and west;
- has indeterminate hand preference;
- performs unevenly from day to day.

BEHAVIOUR

The child:

- employs work avoidance tactics, such as sharpening pencils and looking for books;
- seems to 'dream', does not seem to listen;
- is easily distracted;
- is the class clown or is disruptive or withdrawn (these are often cries for help);
- is excessively tired due to amount of concentration and effort required.

If the child has a cluster of these difficulties together with some abilities they may be dyslexic. Your next step should be to consult the school's Special Educational Needs Co-ordinator immediately to implement action. Never leave it! No child grows out of dyslexia.

Do remember to tell the specialists that the child had a problem with hearing when they were younger. If they are unaware of the connection (after all, it is a new concept) do show them this book!

Pupils in secondary school

Look for the learner who is struggling, despite clear ability in specific aspects of the curriculum. Is this a young person struggling with aspects of reading, writing, spelling and perhaps numeracy? Is this someone who appears not to be able to follow your speech and possibly feels that those around them are speaking too quickly? Does this person have problems learning foreign languages, mathematical tables or even reading musical notation? Does this person tire or lose concentration more quickly than you might expect?

How do you know whether or not a particular adolescent may be dyslexic? What should you look for?

Dyslexia is a combination of abilities as well as difficulties. It is the disparity between them that is often the giveaway. The person who, despite certain areas of difficulty, may still be creative, artistic, sporting or orally very able and knowledgeable. However, alongside these abilities, will be a cluster of difficulties – individual for each person.

WRITTEN WORK

Look out for the learner who:

- has a poor standard of written work compared with oral ability;

- has poor handwriting with badly formed letters;

- has neat handwriting, but writes very slowly indeed;

- produces badly set out or messily written work, with spellings crossed out several times;

- spells the same word differently in one piece of work;

- has difficulty with punctuation and/or grammar;

- confuses upper and lower case letters;

- writes a great deal but 'loses the thread';

- writes very little, but to the point;

- has difficulty taking notes in lessons;

- has difficulty with organisation or even remembering aspects of homework;

- finds tasks difficult to complete on time;

- appears to know more than can be committed to paper.

READING

Look out for the learner who:

- is hesitant and laboured, especially when reading aloud;

- omits, repeats or adds extra words;

- reads at a reasonable rate, but has a low level of comprehension;

- fails to recognise familiar words;

- misses a line or repeats the same line twice;

- loses his place – or uses a finger or marker to keep the place;

- has difficulty in pin-pointing the main idea in a passage;

- has difficulty using dictionaries, directories, encyclopaedias effectively.

NUMERACY

Look out for the learner who:

- has difficulty remembering tables and/or basic number sets;

- finds sequencing problematic;

- confuses signs such as x for +;

- can think at a high level in mathematics, but needs a calculator for simple calculations;

- misreads questions that include words;

- finds mental arithmetic at speed very difficult;

- finds memorising formulae difficult.

OTHER AREAS

Look out for the learner who:

- confuses direction – left/right;
- finds map reading challenging;
- has poor spatial awareness;
- has difficulty in learning foreign languages;
- has indeterminate hand preference;
- has difficulty in finding the name for an object;
- has clear processing problems at speed;
- misunderstands complicated questions;
- finds holding a list of instructions in memory difficult, although can perform all tasks when told individually.

BEHAVIOUR

Look out for the learner who:

- is disorganised or forgetful, e.g. over sports equipment, lessons, homework, appointments;
- is immature and/or clumsy;
- has difficulty relating to others: is unable to 'read' body language;
- is often in the wrong place at the wrong time;
- is excessively tired, due to the amount of concentration and effort required.

If the child has a cluster of these difficulties together with some abilities they may be dyslexic. Your next step should be to consult the school's Special Educational Needs Co-ordinator immediately to implement action. Never leave it! No child grows out of dyslexia.

Do remember to tell the specialists that the child had a problem with hearing when they were younger. If they are unaware of the connection (after all, it is a new concept) do show them this book!

9 **General and specific teaching strategies for the classroom**

In the 'whole class' situation

As most parents are not aware of the connection between early hearing difficulties and learning weaknesses, if teachers have concerns about a child they should ask parents if there is a history of glue ear.

Parents know their children very well. In my experience, if a parent thinks a child has a problem they are generally correct. Furthermore, there may well be a difference in behaviour between home and school. Teachers need to be aware of what is happening in both places to get a full picture of what is happening to any particular child.

Teachers often feel that they do not have time to treat any one child differently from the rest when they have a large number in the class. However, the techniques described below can be used for the whole class. All children will benefit and those that experience specific problems will benefit most of all – in fact it could be said that without the use of such techniques these children will be at a significant disadvantage. None of the following suggestions are at a financial cost to a school and all are easy to implement.

Some learners who have experienced glue ear will find perception of certain sounds problematic, long after the bouts of glue ear have passed. These children may also evidence a series of reactions which may include:

- apparently not listening to instructions;

- not remembering information although apparently understanding the subject;

- confusing the order of tasks;

- mis-spelling words, some of which had apparently already been mastered;

- looking blank when language is spoken at speed.

You may find the following techniques useful:

1. Speak clearly, without shouting.

2. Turn towards the child when you speak so that their eyes are at the level of your face. Get the younger ones to consciously look at your nose and unwittingly they will learn to lip read.

3. Use a structured, sequential, multisensory teaching approach to learning and teaching.

4. Give work which is intellectually stimulating, but has an appropriate literacy level.

5. Ensure the child is stimulated by using a range of techniques which include technological equipment, drama, discussion and visual aids.

6. Ensure that over-learning takes place. If a learner misunderstands, try a variety of techniques to reinforce that which is being taught.

7. Employ small, sequential steps which have been taught systematically.

8. Use a range of learning and teaching styles and allow for difference.

9. If the learner has a strong learning style, it might be useful to put a note on the desk as an indicator for you. For example, an eye, an ear or a hand will act as reminders to anyone working with the child.

10. Encourage staff to show understanding and empathy rather than sympathy.

11. Try not to permit the child to use their learning difficulty as an excuse for lack of trying or success, but rather as a challenge. This will only work if schools provide appropriate support and care.

12. In order to help allay anxiety, teachers might take responsibility for the learner not understanding. Try telling the child that when they do not understand, it is the teacher's responsibility to ensure that he or she finds a method of teaching the way the child learns best; it is never their fault for not understanding. This allows the child to retain self-respect and hopefully remain buoyant whilst teachers find alternative ways to explain.

13. Give children games to play to help develop memory and language competences. Their capabilities need to be fostered.

14. Allow them time to do the piece of set work. Allow for repetition and practice. If the child runs over the end of a lesson, do not take away free time. They need their breaks. Instead, adjust the demands on that particular child – either the quantity or the complexity.

15. Teach the child how to prioritise their tasks and their homework.

16. Teach them how to manage their time. Give them skills to use at home and in school.

17. Present information to them in a variety of ways. Different children will respond to different techniques.

18. Employ a marking system which allows children to succeed even if their written work is not yet up to standard. The child should receive a mark which reflects their knowledge of the subject. The teacher should note the fact that the child's spelling, punctuation and grammar are still below par and need attention. If the school does not act in this way, such children will always receive poor marks and ultimately are likely to become demotivated.

19. Use technological support to enhance teaching if the child will benefit.

20. Ensure there is a 'study buddy' in the class for the child who is struggling.

Teachers should remember that many strategies which are shown to be useful for these pupils will be of benefit to all learners in their classrooms. The problem is that without them, these children are likely to seriously underachieve.

If there is concern about a child, the following considerations may be worth some reflection.

1. If some lessons have been successful, which approaches facilitate success?

2. When is the learner able to remember and learn effectively?

3. Is it possible to analyse together with the learner what makes successful learning and what makes for anxiety and failure in a range of circumstances?

4. Is the environment conducive to learning?

5. Are the surroundings quiet? This is critical for the success of glue ear children.

6. Is the learner facing the teacher when you speak?

7. Is the learner sitting away from auditory and visual distractions? If the child is working in a group, ensure those in the group are focused as well as the children who are sitting on tables nearby.

8. Ensure that a left-handed child is not seated on the right of a right-handed child.

9. Is there sufficient light for the learner to see well? Visual clues will be particularly important for these learners.

10. Use colour and good spacing on the board to ensure that should the child not be able to hear sufficiently well to follow, they will have a visual back-up.

11. Give clear instructions and reinforce where appropriate.

12. Ensure that the teacher can see the learner's eyes so that it is clear to you when something has not been understood.

13. Do not talk with your back to the class or even to the side.

14. If other members of the class are speaking, indicate to this child where the speaker is sitting. They are likely to lose the gist of debate and discussion if they are unable to see faces.

15. Ensure that presented work is at the front of the classroom and is static.

16. Keep copying tasks to a minimum.

17. Do not dictate copious amounts of notes; give transcripts or photocopies where possible.

18. If children have to write notes and certain children cannot do so, give carbon paper to another child – one who writes neatly and clearly – and ask them to make a copy for the one who needs it. This has two benefits:

    ■ the child who finds it hard to write has a good set of notes to take home from which to revise; and

    ■ the child who has difficulty can focus totally on that which you are saying. This allows for maximum concentration.

19. Plan time appropriately. Remember that these children will take longer to process and complete tasks. They should not be kept in at break to complete work if they have not finished in time.

20. Adjust demands of the day to the needs of the child.

21. Label and organise equipment for all children.

22. Ensure that safety regulations in, e.g. science laboratories, are well understood and remembered. Do not rely on the ability to read and comprehend well. In an emergency, language spoken at speed may not be understood either.

23. Encourage drawing of graphs, diagrams, charts and pictures to exemplify ideas.

24. Have plenty of rough paper available for trials in all subject areas.

25. Have spare equipment available – particularly before public examinations.

26. Mark work with the child. Explain to the child what was correct and why they have been praised.

27. Break down all marking and show all parts that are correct as well as any small errors. For example, the word 'plentifull' was 'almost spelt correctly'. It is frustrating for children who have worked hard to succeed to be told they have failed completely for one error, e.g. explain to the child that it was 'almost' correct. Tell them that the suffix 'ful' will only have one 'l' at the end of a word, as opposed to 'll' when in a one-syllable word such as 'full'. Then congratulate them on getting the rest of the word right! With logic and explanation given to them, they are likely to be in a better position later to remember.

PREPARING READABLE WORKSHEETS

Some people find it challenging to understand the information they read for a range of reasons. There are some simple things we can do in school to help when preparing materials. Everyone will benefit.

1. Materials and presentation
   (a) Use coloured paper: off-white takes away the glare.
   (b) Use paper that is matt to reduce glare.
   (c) Use a minimum font size of 12; preferably 14.
   (d) Use 1.5 spacing between lines rather than single spacing.
   (e) Keep lines left justified with a ragged right edge.
   (f) If the individual has problems reading the width of a page, columns will be more accessible.
   (g) Leave space on the page to separate out important pieces of information, questions etc.
   (h) Avoid dense blocks of text.

2. Writing style and accessibility
   (a) Avoid passive sentences. Write in a direct style. For example, 'The boy broke the window' is easier to understand than 'The window was broken by the boy'.
   (b) Give instructions clearly. You want to know whether the learner has understood the work, not the question!
   (c) Keep sentences as clear and precise as possible.
   (d) When giving source materials, ensure that they can be easily read. Enlarging on a photocopier may be necessary.
   (e) Use Mind Maps© and other visual techniques.
   (f) Give a list of technical terms, abbreviations and other words key to understanding the text.

3. Readability

    Teachers are often unaware that the materials they generate for learners are sometimes beyond their comprehension, not because they are intellectually incapable but because they are unable to read effectively. This is particularly the case in secondary schools where there is an assumption that as children can read, all books and worksheets must be fine.

In order to prepare materials appropriate to age, teachers can use a program available on Microsoft Word which will help.

When the program finishes checking spelling and grammar, it displays information about the reading level of the document – including its readability score. This is based on the average number of syllables per word, and words per sentence.

To check readability, go to Tools, Options, Spelling and Grammar, then mark Readability. It will show you:

■ the percentage of passive sentences;

■ a reading ease score; and

■ a grade level score (the grade referring to year at school).

For those of you who are interested, type in a few GCSE and A level questions and see what comes out!!

It is critical that questions and text are written in a format that is accessible to all. By so doing, learners will be in a position to show more of what they know.

STRATEGIES TO HELP CHILDREN REMEMBER:

■ Use a Walkman in class and encourage its use at home to help children remember when rote learning.

■ Use tape recorders to ensure that children hear their own voices. This helps them to remember better.

■ Use games for memorising.

■ Encourage children to teach each other which will reinforce learning and memorisation.

■ Use clues, glossaries and word banks.

■ Use the following tools for various tasks and help the children identify which methods they find most useful: flash cards, visual images, music and rhythm, kinaesthetic tasks, mnemonics.

■ Teach spelling through: 'Read, say, cover, say again, then write, check'.

At the end of the day, some children will still forget, but the techniques will work for most – some of the time!

READING

1. If the child has severe problems reading, you may need to allow a reader in certain circumstances.

2. The use of text on tape is very helpful. Many secondary school children find taped literature very useful – and often enjoyable – so that they can listen or listen and annotate at the same time if they need to.

3. Reduce the amount of reading they have to do if they are still struggling.

4. Encourage paired reading at home and at school.

WRITING

1. Teach the children how to make a plan before they start to write. They should learn a variety of techniques and select one or two with which they feel comfortable.

2. If a child cannot write and make themselves understood, you may have to consider a scribe.

3. With younger children, encourage them to present their work in a range of ways. For example, comic strips, taped stories, story boards.

4. Some children produce better work when word processing.

5. Teach children the use of writing frames and scaffolding.

SPELLING

1. Help the children devise their own personal dictionary and carry it with them.

2. Put word banks around the room.

3. If children have severe spelling problems, allow them to use a spellchecker.

4. Allow children to ask at an appropriate moment if they need help.

5. In order to help children to develop their skills in spelling, use as many rules as possible.

6. Help them to separate syllables and words. One method uses a hand under the chin to 'feel' syllables . . . the chin drops each time a syllable is spoken.

7. Allow more time in order to help children to develop their skills in spelling.

It is vital that these children are helped to develop speech, communication and language. As they have not had the opportunity of good early hearing and often do not choose to read, their language and vocabulary skills are often weak.

Handwriting can be improved for younger children. For those in secondary schools, neatness often is created at the expense of speed. When starting, use cursive script. The worst thing for these children is to have to learn one way of writing, then have to unlearn and relearn. Start the way you mean to go on!

SELF-ESTEEM

1. Develop the learner's confidence by reinforcing each step of the learning process. The child will then develop the desire to tackle work that is challenging without fear of failure.

2. Use very specific praise so that the child is aware of why they were good or successful. Surprisingly this sometimes has to be spelt out.

3. Be totally consistent with demands. In a secondary school situation this is harder as various teachers have differing requirements and standards. Each one should make themselves clear to the child.

4. Find the fine balance between helping too much and not helping enough. Eventually the child will need to be empowered to cope alone. Use your judgement as to when the time is right.

5. Reward the child by reading out their work or hanging it on the wall. Some of these children report that they are never praised.

6. Foster their strengths and highlight their abilities. They are very aware of their weaknesses and failings. They need to be proud of their strengths.

7. Expect that there will be an inconsistency in levels of attention and motivation.

Never:

- highlight their weaknesses or errors in front of anyone else;

- allow them to be humiliated by anyone;

- allow name calling; that is the beginning of bullying;

- ask them to do anything that will embarrass them.

Be aware of the need for social skills development. Behaviour is sometimes cited as problematic in these children. Often it is as a result of not hearing clearly, not processing quickly enough or not understanding non-verbal communication. This needs to be noted and skills need to be developed as importantly as academic skills.

When an understanding of the full impact of the condition has taken place and appropriate steps are taken for support, the learner's self-esteem and motivation will grow. Success will then become a self-fulfilling prophecy.

More specific strategies

This is a look at the specific needs of these children above and beyond the general strategies used in the class.

LISTENING AND LANGUAGE STRATEGIES

If the school is lucky enough to have a Sound Field System, these children are likely to improve dramatically. The system will allow the child to hear clearly from whatever part of the classroom that they may be in. This is likely to have a profound calming effect too as they will not have to strain as much to hear, follow and concentrate. As these systems are costly it is highly unlikely that you will have access to one, unless you happen to work at a school where there are profoundly deaf children. Enough of blue skies thinking!

TECHNIQUES WHICH WILL HELP LEARNERS

Decide which techniques are appropriate for the individual and for their age and stage in the learning process. These ideas are based on and developed from research findings of Roberts and Wallace (1999). They are all at no financial cost!

1. Make your speech louder or clearer.
2. Get down on child's level to talk to them.
3. Speak to them and use visual and auditory aids to augment that which you are saying.
4. Gain child's attention before speaking.
5. Remind child to listen before you start speaking.
6. Speak clearly using natural intonation.
7. Repeat important words for emphasis.
8. When there is a speaker in the classroom, seat the child close to the speaker but where he can also see the other children's faces.
9. Minimise background noise.
10. Reduce distractions by using moveable barriers for small group and 1:1 work.
11. Hang curtains over windows to absorb sound.
12. Close doors and windows if there is noise outside.
13. Engage in child's discussions and interests.
14. Play interactive games.
15. Model desired language by describing on-going activities.
16. Respond immediately and consistently to child's attempts to converse.
17. Pause to give the child time to talk; time is the greatest gift a teacher can give these learners.
18. Check with child to see that everything has been understood.
19. Elaborate on child's speech by adding words.
20. Encourage discussions on any topic that will engage the child, either academic or emotional.
21. Increase the child's awareness of the use of vocabulary and grammatical rules.
22. Provide a rich environment as a stimulus for the child.
23. Sing simple songs with repeated words and phrases.
24. Play word and listening games.
25. Play rhyming games.
26. Read frequently with children, labelling and describing pictures.

Do not forget that the learner is likely to be left with difficulties even once they have grown out of the stage of suffering bouts of the condition.

- Expect the young person to have difficulties discriminating in a noisy background.

- Remember that concentration may be impaired.

- Foreign language learning may be problematic.

- Processing written and spoken language may be slow.

- Spelling difficulties may be evident.

- Tiredness may be evident as they have to exert a great deal of effort listening and attending.

Strategies specifically related to the secondary school curriculum

Secondary school teachers are never told about hearing problems suffered some years prior to entry to the school. It is worth asking parents about this as they are unlikely to realise that the information will be of any benefit! In addition to the information above, some cost-free techniques are outlined below. These might be of value in subject-specific areas.

METACOGNITIVE AWARENESS

In all subject areas, people need to know *how* to learn. For those who have little problem with learning, it may seem an odd statement. However, for these learners as well as many others it is critical that they are taught in a way that clarifies their needs and actions. They are often impulsive workers who 'jump in' and start working with little thought for direction and outcome. To get them to question themselves and think before they start is always a good technique. What are the six questions they should ask?

- Purpose: Why am I doing this?

- Outcome: What is the required end product?

- Strategy: What strategy should be used?

- Monitoring: Was it successful?

- Development: How can it be improved?

- Transfer: Can it be transferred to another situation?

If teachers encourage pupils to do this before they start their work and then assess the outcome of their efforts, academic leaps are much more likely.

These learners are likely to have some difficulties within all areas of the curriculum:

ORGANISATION AND TIME KEEPING

Organisation is likely to be one of the main areas of weakness that causes great difficulty at secondary school. It affects learning both at home and at school and in some instances can interfere with a person's social life as well. Ensure that the learner has a good sense of time before giving tasks that are time related. There are those who use a digital watch and can read you the numbers, but actually have little concept of what can actually be achieved in a specific time frame.

Difficulties may be apparent in a whole range of ways. For example, when trying to plan homework and organise a revision schedule; when planning what to pack in the school bag for the next day; remembering when and where they should be at any particular time; trying to identify keys point of study for learning. Any number of situations may cause a great deal of stress and anxiety.

Strategies that may help include:

1. A teacher writing out the main points of the lesson and the homework as the class begins. This could be copied by the student in their own time; could be given to them on a sheet of paper by the teacher; could be produced on carbon paper by a 'buddy'.

2. Allowing the student sufficient time to ask questions if the homework is not clearly understood.

3. Have an A4 sized plastic envelope 'living' in the student's bag which is used for carrying homework and handouts to and from school.

4. Have a filing system set up at home whereby each subject has its own file. Agree with parents that the learner will file their paperwork as they arrive home, in the correct place.

5. Teach a 'bring forward' system of work for the learner in order to be able to plan their work.

6. Employ diaries on a yearly, weekly and daily basis. Teach students how best to fill these in using colour and forward planning.

7. For the person who loses their way around the school, produce a map using colour.

8. Encourage students to exchange telephone numbers with their peers so that they can speak at home if something is forgotten.

9. If the school has an intranet system, post all homework so that the learner can view it externally.

10. Ask parents to encourage children to pack their bags the night before school.

COMMITTING IDEAS TO PAPER

It is well known that these learners know a great deal more in their heads than they are able to commit to paper. Teachers might like to try some of the following techniques:

1. Use Mind Mapping© or other visual displays to exemplify key points.

2. Avoid dictation and give key ideas in frameworks.

3. Talk through their ideas in pairs or groups to help cement their thinking.

4. Encourage these children to hold their own personal dictionaries with their subject-specific bank of words.

5. For those who will be using laptops in examinations, encourage them to use them in school. For others, encourage writing in class and the use of laptops at home (where possible) so that work is well organised and better expressed.

6. Encourage them to listen to their own work on tape. This will help with proof-reading.

ENGLISH

1. Encourage reluctant readers to enjoy literature on tape. This will improve their vocabulary and allow them to take a full part of the class in class discussions.

2. Encourage them to use highlighter pens to mark key words and points.

3. Encourage students to try and read ahead of the class so that they are well prepared for discussion on the topic.

4. For those who cannot write effectively, allow the use of tapes or computers.

5. If they are studying literature, viewing of the story on video might help – particularly if the text is in Olde English.

6. Give frameworks to structure writing.

MODERN FOREIGN LANGUAGES

1. Teach using multisensory methodologies.

2. Employ as many memory techniques as possible to help reinforce learning of vocabulary.

3. Teach spelling and grammatical rules where possible.

4. Present all information visually and orally.

5. Encourage the use of colour for highlighting wherever possible.

6. If the teacher's accent is not a native one, there may be need for application to the Examination Boards for the class teacher to speak to the learner in the accent that they recognise. Glue ear will sometimes make it impossible to understand a new accent and the speed of the native spoken voice. A doctor's letter may be necessary to accompany the school request.

HISTORY, PSHE AND RE

1. Chronological order of events in history may prove challenging. Visual presentation may help.

2. The use of video/real life interview may bring alive the subject area.

3. Give a word bank in the subject-specific area.

4. Encourage the use of Mind Maps© and other visual techniques.

5. Put some of the written sources onto tape rather than demanding a heavy reading load on the learner if they are unable to cope with it.

6. Bullet point key ideas and words for focus.

GEOGRAPHY

1. Use models and or videos where possible.

2. Remember that these learners may confuse signs, symbols and numbers. Use those as exemplars that are less likely to confuse the learner, e.g. 25 and 52.

3. Use Mind Maps© and other visuals to organise information.

4. Use highlighters to identify key words and ideas.

5. Give a word bank in the subject-specific area.

6. Take learners on trips outside to experience as many of the geographical features as possible.

MATHEMATICS

1. Remember that learners may have poor memories for formulae and tables but be excellent mathematicians. Therefore provide table squares and calculators if and where appropriate. Remember too that they might confuse signs, e.g. +/x.

2. Ensure that sufficient time is given for oral mathematics. It will take more time than others for glue ear learners to hear and process that which is spoken.

3. Ensure that squared paper is offered for those still experiencing weaknesses in sequencing.

4. Ensure that the learners are cognisant of the language used for the same words, e.g. add, sum, total. Give subject specific dictionaries.

5. If they are evidencing problems relating to spatial awareness, give them opportunities to experience by handling objects.

6. Ensure that their knowledge of early mathematics is in place before attempting to build on this work at a higher conceptual level.

SCIENCES

1. Ensure that they understand the rules of safety in the science laboratory.

2. Some learners will have problems reading scientific vocabulary. As such offer word banks, labels and a subject-specific personal dictionary.

3. Ask them to repeat back instructions to ensure they have understood that which they need to do.

4. Use Mind Maps© and other visual ways of recording experiments.

5. Provide notes wherever possible so that they can focus on you and on the experiment and take good notes home for revision and homework.

6. Provide coloured markers for organising steps in any process. Remember that they might confuse signs e.g. +/x. Ensure they know what they are doing.

DESIGN AND TECHNOLOGY

1. Ensure that they understand the rules of safety in the science laboratory.

2. Help the learners organise themselves, their equipment and the space around them.

3. Speak slowly and clearly ensuring that all instructions are clearly understood.

4. If the learner has fine motor skills weaknesses, it will take them significantly longer to fulfil a task than others.

5. Ensure that they understand and can manage small measurements.

6. If they need to work to a tight time scale, ensure that they are given an appropriate amount of work to do in that time.

ART AND DESIGN

1. Some learners may forget the order of tasks they have to do. Either draw them out or write them down so that they can follow sequentially.

2. Have a small dictionary or bank of subject-specific words.

3. When researching on the internet, ensure that they understand and can reproduce in their own words. Use frameworks for structure.

4. Use a range of visual aids for a range of tasks.

5. They may copy words or images in the wrong order. If so, help them reorganise.

6. Mark for effort if they find great difficulty manipulating their hands to produce work.

PE

1. Organisation is likely to be a problem for some learners. Allow them sufficient time to organise themselves and for changing clothes.

2. There may be confusion between left and right. Point with your hands to show which direction you mean them to go.

3. If they have difficulty remembering a sequence of tasks, instructions, movements, give them the information in small tasks.

4. Teach them the terminology by providing visual images where possible.

5. Encourage the use of diagrams and visuals for recording work.

6. In examination preparation, teach them how to break down tasks into manageable steps.

MUSIC

1. These learners may have the same problems reading music as they do reading language. Use a range of multisensory techniques to ensure acquisition of musical notation.

2. Use highlighters to colour code individual notes.

3. If they have a problem with the direction of the notes, put stickers at the left hand side of the page so that they know where to start.

4. Glue ear learners may have difficulty hearing pitch and tone. Teach in small manageable chunks and, possibly, using louder notes than you might otherwise do.

5. Have a small dictionary of bank of subject-specific words.

6. Enlarge the music so that it is clearer to read.

10 Issues of self-esteem

I have had the opportunity to work with many children and adolescents with learning disorders during the past thirty years. In conducting therapy with these youths, I became increasingly aware that most were burdened by feelings of low self-worth and incompetence and that many believed that their situation would not improve. Not surprisingly, this sense of hopelessness served as a major obstacle to future success. Once children believe that things will not improve, they are likely to engage in self-defeating ways of coping such as quitting or avoiding tasks, blaming others for their difficulties, or becoming class clowns or bullies. Thus a negative cycle is often set in motion, intensifying feelings of defeat and despair.

(Brooks, 2001)

Behavioural problems

Often dyslexic learners will evidence behavioural problems in school. Unfortunately some educationalists still consider behaviour as the root cause of the learning difficulty rather than the result of it. Children may behave poorly due to the fact that they are:

- misunderstood;
- badly handled;
- misdiagnosed;
- underestimated.

Any of these situations may well lead to frustration, anger, low motivation and low self-esteem.

When asked how they see their future, adolescent learners report feelings of insecurity, unhappiness at being labelled lazy, fear of ridicule and of humiliation. Their teachers may describe them as often appearing to have regressed and show signs of immaturity for their years.

Stress

Stress leads to anxiety and in some cases to aggression. What are the manifestations of stress? These may be wide ranging.

The most common are:

- poor concentration;

- headaches;
- insomnia;
- disordered vision – elusive eye problems;
- neckaches;
- difficulty with swallowing;
- eating disorders;
- high blood pressure;
- breathing problems;
- less resistance to infection;
- allergies;
- school phobia.

Additionally in the case of dyslexic learners, stress and low self-esteem may manifest itself by:

- rudeness to parents and or teachers;
- hyper-reactivity (Peer and Reid, 2000);
- running away from school;
- fooling about in school . . . the class clown;
- threat of suicide.

It must be recognised that if dyslexia is not diagnosed and appropriately dealt with, barriers to advancement may persist into adult life. This may well cause frustration, anger and depression.

DOES STRESS CAUSE DYSLEXIA?

Absolutely not! Stress will cause a reduction in functioning across the curriculum and not in *specific* areas; dyslexia is a *specific* learning difficulty. That is to say that some areas will be affected and others will not. Stress will undoubtedly make things worse and be the cause of poorer functioning in examination conditions.

AT HOME

Parents are left to deal with the after effects that stress causes at school. Many parents will identify the fact that something is wrong long before it is noticed in school. They will sense the frustration in their child and try and cope with it alone. Other parents deny the problem feeling that failure reflects on them. Dyslexia is the fault of no-one and no blame should be apportioned.

APPROPRIATE INTERVENTION

In order to prevent this demise into low self-esteem with its accompanying negative consequences, there is a need to identify and intervene as early as possible.

Appropriate provision should ensure that such learners go on to become successful adults. Academic weakness is only part of the glue ear/dyslexic profile. It is of great concern that even with today's knowledge, many people indeed still do experience that which Brooks outlined above. It is up to both parents and educationalists to prevent this from happening. The socio-emotional needs of any learner are as important as academic needs. In fact it is true to say that if needs other than the academic are not met, serious obstacles to general success will be faced.

Ten strategies for boosting self-esteem

A range of strategies should be in place to encourage changes in behaviour. There are no magic wands! The longer the person has had feelings of low self-esteem, the longer it seems to take to overcome the problem. It is also very important that the learner knows that it is not their fault if they cannot learn, but the job of the teacher to find a way to ensure they do!

- Discuss targets with the child and with the parents.
- Set small, achievable tasks.
- Agree positive and negative consequences.
- Sit the learner with a good role model.
- Recognise appropriate contributions; ignore those that are not!
- Read out the person's work; hang a corrected script on the wall.
- If the learner is avoiding working, assess whether or not he can actually do the work. Is it beyond them? Check with the specialist teacher.
- Use the learner's strengths wherever possible – so that peers see the strengths that person has.
- Teach self-control (learning a martial art can help).
- Teach them to work co-operatively.

Teachers know that how they present knowledge and information to these learners will determine their absorption of it. If, for example, we are predominantly auditory learners ourselves and only teach in the way we learn best, those in our classes who may better absorb information in a visual way will find themselves at a great disadvantage. No wonder some learners tell their parents that they hate the very subject they loved the previous year! It is not about the subject; it is about the way it is delivered. Dare I say that for those with the mildest of difficulties, I might ask whether a depiction of the problem might be specific *teaching* difficulties as opposed to specific *learning* difficulties?

EMPATHY NOT SYMPATHY

Goleman (1995) speaks of the need for empathy. This is highly relevant in relation to these learners. There are those who prefer to ignore dyslexia altogether or at the other extreme, those who are sympathetic. Neither of these responses is appropriate. Understanding, together with structure, support and encouragement are the most useful responses. All learners – including those who appear to experience difficulty with the commitment of information onto paper – have areas of strength. Many dyslexic people are highly creative in the visual arts, others in computing, yet others orally. Self-esteem will improve once strengths are identified and encouraged to flourish. Helping out another student can be a valuable confidence booster: encourage good two-way 'buddy systems' wherever possible.

Dyslexic learners need to have goals that they can achieve. Small steps that are explicit and measurable are most effective, both academically and emotionally.

Dyslexic adults have reported that for them, success is achieving their dream in terms of a career, being able to function as literate and numerate people and being able to accept positive criticism and deal with negative criticism. When asked what made this possible, responses were that they had parents and teachers who believed in them and as such they saw their dyslexia as a challenge rather than as a nightmare. Perhaps the answer is that they saw themselves as having learning *differences* rather than learning *difficulties*.

Some dyslexic learners will do well in a 'dyslexia-friendly' school. This will be most appropriate for those with mild to moderate difficulties. However, those with more severe needs will undoubtedly need more specialist help; this may or may not be possible in a dyslexia-friendly school.

Teachers must take responsibility for all children in their care, across the curriculum. Class and subject teachers, working with the SENCo and support staff, can ensure that dyslexic learners fulfil their potential, achieve their inidividual targets and help the school to reach its goals!

11 Listening to the children

The information below was collected as part of a project on dyslexia-friendly schools. The children's comments make a fascinating read!

One hundred and thirty eight children completed questionnaires – from both primary and secondary schools. The pupils were encouraged to fill in the questionnaires with the help of their parents but to respond using their own words. They were asked to think about teachers, classes and schools in their own experience.

QUESTION 1

This asked about the characteristics of a teacher from whom they might easily learn.

Primary pupils said:

- At the start of a lesson a teacher should make it clear exactly what she wants us to do.
- Show us, don't just tell us.
- Give us time to listen.
- It is easier if the teacher is enthusiastic.
- The use of pictures and materials make it easier to understand.
- We like to be able to ask questions and to have teachers check that we are doing the right thing.
- Good teachers give help if you 'get stuck' and are patient if you need things repeated.
- Teachers should be nice, should not shout if you get things wrong. They should be patient with your mistakes.

Nearly half of the responses of the secondary school pupils also related to being understanding, ready to spend time helping, explaining things carefully, proactively checking, repeating instructions and explanations, and being ready to answer questions. They made comments such as:

- Explain, then ask if I understood, if not, explain with pictures, etc. But if I do understand, then don't overdo it so that it becomes boring.
- Good teachers aren't ignorant and unsociable people. They notice when you are having problems and they don't dismiss you by ignoring you and your questions.

Next came the use of handouts, writing instructions clearly and carefully on the board (preferably a white board) and ensuring that students had a homework diary.

■ A good teacher writes things down clearly and just writes and teaches the basic information without rambling on about other things.

Only after these crucial elements have been provided do they mention making lessons fun and practical, giving time to think and write and encouraging and rewarding good attempts.

■ When I am stuck I know I can put my hand up and not get shouted at for not listening. The teacher smiles at me and then explains it again, doing at least two examples with me.

It is interesting that again personal characteristics were all seen as more important than the provision of support materials. Good support includes putting and leaving instructions and spellings on a large white board or personal 'crib-sheet', putting homework instructions on tape, allowing oral or taped responses etc. The overall impression is quite clear – pupils with dyslexia need teachers who are clear and concise, pleasant with their classes and prepared to recognise that not everyone understands the first time.

QUESTION 2

This was the reverse of Question 1 and asked about the characteristics of teachers from whom it was difficult to learn. Nearly half the primary pupils said that they gave too many instructions too fast, didn't check if you understood and didn't allow you to ask questions. Time itself was important too. Pupils also needed time to do their work – particularly if it involved writing. Ineffective teachers:

■ rush you – they tell you off if you don't get enough done;

■ don't let you think long enough before making you start work;

■ say you have a time limit for something and you want to make it a good piece of work and then you have to finish it off badly by saying something like 'Happily ever after!'

For a third of the pupils the main complaint was shouting and they were clear about the effects on their learning:

■ They shout all the time for no apparent reason.

■ The teacher getting into a stress when I get something wrong results in disruption of my ability to think.

■ When she shouts a lot it makes it hard to think; you can't concentrate.

■ If I get told off it sticks in my head and I can't concentrate on my work.

The second complaint was being shown up in front of the class:

■ like being asked aloud in class how many I got correct in my spelling test;

■ ask you to do things that they know you will fail at;

■ one teacher told the whole class I wasn't doing very well and I felt embarrassed and really couldn't think.

One in five complained about work on the board and displays generally. These included not being able to see the board, teacher writing on the board and then rubbing it out too soon or standing in front of it. One teacher:

- Put the number line at the back of the class and then told me off if I turned round to look at it!

For the secondary pupils, two categories were most frequent – teachers who don't give you enough time and teachers who make you copy from the board or a book. Feeling rushed is probably a very good indicator that all is not right with the teaching and learning process rather than a direct cause in itself.

Again, resorting to the very ineffective method of just getting pupils to copy down information is a feature of poor teaching generally. This is confirmed by the next most frequent category – talking too much or too fast. Taking these categories together they cover a third of all the responses.

The next complaints were

- can't control the class;
- shouts all the time;
- puts you down;
- doesn't explain.

QUESTION 3

This asked what subject they found most difficult because of their dyslexia.

Three subjects were identified by a significant number of primary pupils – English, maths and science. The reasons, unsurprisingly, related to literacy – writing, spelling and reading being mentioned in that order. English was again the most frequently mentioned by over half the secondary pupils. Maths, modern foreign languages (MFL), science and humanities followed, each mentioned by about one in three. Reasons given tended to relate to curriculum delivery rather than content or process. Overemphasis on grammar, spelling and punctuation was the main complaint, followed by the need for writing or having to take dictation, too much reading or having to remember facts or formulae. The only actual criticism of a subject was directed at MFL.

- I can't spell in English so spelling in French and Spanish is madness.
- I find it hard to spell and I don't understand tenses and punctuation. I can barely understand English so French is worse.

Interestingly some students disclaimed any problems:

- In secondary school I do not find any subject too difficult – I like a challenge. In primary school however I found maths hard. This is probably because we (the class and I) were forced to do many timed tests (mainly mental arithmetic) approximately four times a week.

Another student felt there were no problems, because all teachers were well informed by the SENCo and an IEP.

In primary school, art was the least affected. Some could cope with maths itself, but the reading and writing associated with it created many problems. PE was the third subject mentioned. There then followed science, music, design and technology and games. The main reason given was that there was little or no writing. They felt they were good at it or that it was a practical, hands-on subject.

This emphasis on the demands that the actual teaching process makes rather than the conceptual nature of the discipline, is even clearer in responses from pupils at secondary schools. The top subjects were art followed by PE. However, again maths, science, humanities and design and technology posed few problems if teachers demanded no writing, presented their subject in a 'practical' way or did not emphasise spelling. There were also comments relating to enjoying the subject: it being made interesting by good teachers, there being appropriate support or that they were prepared to work particularly hard.

- I like them (sic) subjects. I have a real interest in them and that overrides my dyslexia.

- We have good teachers and science and history you can think through.

- My dyslexia helps me to think in a different way.

QUESTION 4

The children were asked what they felt were the worst effects on school life generally of being dyslexic.

Nearly one-third of the responses from primary school pupils related to feeling stupid or different and/or not knowing as much as the others. Some of this is brought about by thoughtlessness:

- You have to ask for spellings all the time if you want to get them right and the teacher writes them on the board which makes the rest of the class think how stupid I am.

- Not being given credit for being as intelligent as others just because I have difficulty in speed of writing and spelling.

- I am never picked to do cool things because I can't read or remember things like everyone else.

Another effect was not being able to write either easily or properly and the problem of working slowly, resulting in certain tasks, particularly homework, 'taking ages'.

The majority of secondary pupils said the main effect was that they couldn't read, write or spell easily and

- being different;
- people don't understand you;
- work takes a long time to complete;
- bullying in one form or another.

Nearly 40 per cent of the children claimed that their dyslexia affected either how they felt about themselves or how others treated them. Judging by the overall quality and cogency of their replies, these pupils and students were well integrated with good self-awareness. They were being made to feel different, sometimes aggressively, in their school situation. In other words – their classrooms were not inclusive. Typical responses were:

- people can do things I can't;
- they can understand things more easily;
- being embarrassed to keep asking for help – going to the special needs group;
- when you are in need of help, people explain things to you as if you are stupid;
- being made to feel stupid in front of my friends;
- teachers saying 'Children like you…';
- letting down my parents (but dad is dyslexic too);
- being followed around by a teaching assistant.

QUESTION 5

This asked the children to tell all teachers something about how to teach pupils with dyslexia. There was a clear consensus amongst all the pupils. More than 80 per cent said that:

- Teachers should explain better in the first place, then check whether pupils had understood.
- They should be prepared to repeat instructions and explanations.
- Talk plainly, clearly and to the child.
- Watch over my shoulder every so often and write spellings in the margin.
- Concentrate on what the person is saying without thinking about what you are going to have for dinner or who's fighting over there.
- They are having a hard time telling the teacher because they are embarrassed.
- They should explain what you have to do as many times as needed; explaining the same way as before if you don't understand is not helpful. They may need to use a different approach.

This was then followed by a request that teachers should not shout, should be patient and should give more time. In other words once instructions have been understood, they should trust pupils to be involved in their work and accept mistakes as genuine attempts at learning. Further:

- Good teachers notice when you are having problems and they don't dismiss you by ignoring you and your questions.
- When I am stuck I know I can put my hand up and not get shouted at for not listening.
- The teacher smiles at me and then explains it again, doing at least two examples with me.

Overall, it is clear that these pupils have no difficulty recognising the learning environment in which they can succeed. It is interesting that the underlying theme is the emotional climate in the classroom rather than any specific techniques or special methodology. They want calmness and security, the feeling that teachers might actually like them and are enthusiastic about their subject, quiet recognition of their difference and the provision of low-key differentiation and support.

This all builds up to a picture that suggests enhancing the achievements of pupils with dyslexia does not make unreasonable demands on teachers at either primary or secondary phases of education. (This does not include those severely affected.) It is the way they go about their teaching and organising classrooms that are seen as either facilitating or frustrating. The key comes in understanding how each pupil thinks and feels.

Children with glue ear are very likely to have experienced specific difficulties in learning. Teachers and assistants must adjust their techniques to meet their needs.

12 Planning for the learner's educational needs

The fact that a child is sitting in a classroom being taught by no means guarantees that they are learning! The learner knows this, but it often takes a long time before teachers and parents become aware. It is fundamentally important that when a learner is not making the progress that they should, provision and monitoring are put in place. It is essential to know that the provision is appropriate and effective and is adapted to need as time passes. All education plans must reflect this on-going change and make adjustment for need as required.

Types of assessment

There are different types of assessment that can be used to assess a learner's strengths and weaknesses, as well as indicate where the child is at any place in time in relation to specific areas of literacy and numeracy.

Reid and Wearmouth (2002) describe the difference between *formative* and *summative* assessment and the links into teaching and learning:

1. Formative assessment is carried out by teachers to collect information and evidence about a pupil's literacy development and to plan the next step in his/her learning. It combines the assessment of skills required for specific tasks . . . where the pupil's progress is tracked across time.

2. Summative assessment takes place at certain intervals when achievement has to be recorded and is intended to provide a global picture of the learner's literacy development to date. It requires a high degree of reliability, and may involve a combination of different types of assessment.

In some cases it may be important to bring in the services and expertise of outside agencies, such as speech and language or occupational therapists.

Parents and learners themselves must be brought into the discussions as far as possible as they too should be taking responsibility for their part in the learning process.

Curriculum factors

Dyslexic learners may try to conceal their difficulties when they see others around them succeeding when they are not. In many cases they may well be aware that others are less knowledgeable, but as they can write better, they will achieve higher marks. This can be very dispiriting.

There are many ways to conceal failure. Montgomery (1998) cites:

■ withdrawal;

■ avoidance;

■ evasion;

■ distraction;

■ digression;

■ disruption;

■ clowning;

■ daydreaming;

■ negativism;

■ absenteeism; and

■ cheating;

■ clowning is a common response of able learners.

WHAT TO PROVIDE?

It is clear that teachers need to offer their dyslexic learners a differentiated curriculum. This is one that both addresses the average to high intellectual potential, but equally addresses lower level literacy (and possibly numeracy) abilities.

If the range of specific learning difficulties, including dyslexia, is not addressed early on, there will be a worsening effect as the years go by. So first, children should be screened for dyslexic-type difficulties and an early intervention programme should be put in place. This is of great help both to the individual and to the coffers!

Designing GEPs and IEPs

Group Education Plans (GEPs) and Individual Education Plans (IEPs) are of great value when providing and monitoring for need.

If the whole class is taught using methodologies as outlined in Chapter 9, those glue ear/dyslexic children who are affected to a mild degree should have their needs met.

There may be a small group of children for whom that level of input is not sufficient. For them a GEP will be of use. These are for children who will receive additional help in a small group on a regular basis. For those who are affected to an even greater degree and whose needs are individual and specific, there will be a need for an IEP. That means that this particular child needs specific support in certain areas, which is not needed by other learners. This is likely to be in addition to work undertaken in the whole group.

Review procedures

The GEP and IEP review meetings will involve a range of people:

- the learner;
- the parent;
- tutor/teacher;
- teaching assistant;
- SENCo;
- external agencies if appropriate;
- head of year (if in a secondary school).

In an ideal world all these people would attend; reality dictates that this rarely happens. If any individual is unable to attend in person, a written/verbal submission should be requested. There should be a place on the GEP/IEP sheet where their comments can be documented.

During the meeting it is important to identify whether it is felt that targets have been met and whether progress has been made; new targets should then be documented. Decisions as to whether further external advice and/or input is required and any updated information should be documented. This information should then be sent to all those working with the learner.

If it is decided that the learner is making good progress and no longer needs extra help, their name can be removed from the special needs record. However, they must continue to be supported through whole class differentiation. Teachers must be aware that taking away support can sometimes inadvertently cause regression. Should there be deterioration in learning or in self-esteem, the child should be placed back on the special needs register with support.

For those requiring on-going support, detailed targets will be necessary both in the GEP and the IEP so that all those involved know what the needs are and how they will be addressed.

If the learner has needs that are not being met and are severe enough to meet the criteria needed for Statutory Assessment, the SENCo should notify parents and refer to the Local Education Authority. In the meantime, the learner should continue to receive help.

13 Working with parents

Parents are understandably concerned when their children seem not to be making the progress in school that they expect. They often see children at home who are bright, aware, happy and able, rapidly becoming miserable and demotivated when placed in an educational environment. They are often aware that it is not anyone's fault in particular, as they know that other children in their families or in the neighbourhood are doing well and are happy. This may cause parents to have feelings of stress, anxiety, guilt, anger and fear.

Many parents will have experienced difficulties themselves in the education process and dread the prospect of their children going through the same 'nightmare'. Parents have told me that just walking into school, they feel their throats tightening as they relive their own past experiences and are fearful for their children. Today, some of these parents are successful in their own fields; yet others feel as though they have not fulfilled their potential. Some parents have only recently discovered the reason for their own past difficulties, through the identification of their children's problems many years later. Some feel relieved; others feel angry at the way they were treated and how they were made to feel about themselves over the years.

Parents are particularly stressed when:

(a) There is tension at home in relation to fights over homework.

(b) There are stresses at home in relation to organisation ... or lack of!

(c) They see that their child is frustrated and disheartened.

(d) Schools do not accept their real concerns.

(e) Teachers state that they do not 'believe' in the existence of dyslexia, or when they say that they know that the child will 'grow out of' the problem. No-one grows out of these types of difficulties.

(f) They have had familial experience of specific learning difficulties which were not addressed successfully.

(g) They are concerned about schooling, transition arrangements and the child's future chances in life.

So what can schools do to help parents?

Many schools will be doing the following as a matter of course; others that are not may benefit from trying this out. The aim is to develop helpful working relationships with parents which will ease the way to greater success for all concerned. When it works:

1. The teacher will feel more in control of the success and achievements of the child.

2. The teacher will see improved behaviour of the child as they feel understood and more successful.

3. The child will feel a sense of academic achievement, and equality with peers, and feel more valued by others.

4. The child will feel more motivated and evidence a growing sense of self-worth.

5. The parent will see a more positive attitude from the child and greater understanding from staff which will give them an increased confidence in the school.

6. Schools work well with parents and there is a greater sense of empowerment for all concerned. This can only lead to a positive outcome.

SUGGESTED ACTIONS

1. If parents appear anxious, schools should accept that there is a reason and recognise that concerns are usually justified.

2. Offer parents solutions and preferably information as to the background of their child's needs. Assure them that the school will do everything possible to help.

3. Ensure that there is regular communication between home and school. Some parents may prefer phone calls as opposed to the written word.

4. Explain to parents that their children will go through screening/testing and/or other assessment procedures to identify any problems. Explain how these will guide parents and staff into the best provision for the child.

5. Assure parents that they will receive objective measures of progress in terms of academia and a subjective review of emotional and social development on a twice-yearly or termly basis.

6. Explain to parents that, following in-house intervention, should the problems continue, the school will take advice from external professionals. Following this they will then work, in tandem with parents if appropriate, to implement any advice given.

7. Assure parents that all staff will be made aware of their child's strengths and weaknesses and that teaching styles will be adjusted to take into consideration the child's learning styles. Further, should greater intervention be necessary, the school will do all it can to ensure that this happens.

8. Assure parents that their children will be offered every opportunity to develop their self-esteem.

9. Explain the system of examination provisions that will be given to the child, if and when appropriate.

10. If the child is ready to move up a stage in the education system, give appropriate advice on the most appropriate schooling. Assure parents that information will be passed onto the next school detailing what has been done to support the child so far and the child's strengths and weaknesses. If possible, allow the child to spend a few hours in the next school, meeting the staff and familiarising themselves with the environment.

11. If the young person is ready to move on into further or higher education, ensure that the institution chosen is able to provide for identified needs and that both parents and learners are given all the information necessary to make the transition happen successfully.

12. If the child is ready to move into the work place, ensure career guidance is given by a person who understands the specific needs of the individual.

Finally: for many, glue ear is a condition that has profound effects on learning. Parents, educators and health visitors need to be appraised of the condition and its implications. Catching these children early and offering appropriate provision will guarantee that success is likely in the long term. I hope that this book is a helpful guide along that path.

Glossary

Auditory discrimination the ability to identify similarities and differences between sounds.

Auditory memory hearing, listening and remembering.

Auditory perception the ability to understand sounds and/or spoken language.

Comprehension the ability to understand.

Conductive hearing loss hearing loss that fluctuates due to glue ear or congestion.

Co-ordination getting the muscles of the body to work together the way they should.

Decoding the ability to interpret that which is written.

Dyslexia a combination of abilities and difficulties that affect the learning process in one or more of reading, spelling and writing. Accompanying weaknesses may be identified in speed of processing, short-term memory, sequencing, organisation and possibly motor skills.

Dyspraxia motor difficulties caused by perceptual problems.

Encoding writing information down.

ENT department Ear, Nose and Throat department at a hospital.

Fluctuating hearing loss hearing tends to come and go. Typical of glue ear difficulties.

GEP Group Education Plan

Glue ear an inflammation of the middle ear.

Grapheme a unit of a writing system that represents one phoneme.

Grommet small plastic tube medically inserted through the ear drum to aid the hearing process when a glue-like fluid blocks the passageways.

IEP Individual Education Plan

Listening comprehension understanding speech. Basic level includes only understanding the facts explicitly stated in a spoken passage. Advanced levels in clued implicit understanding and inferences from passages that are more complex in nature.

Magnocellular visual and auditory pathways to the part of the brain called the thalamus.

Memory (a) short-term memory – remembering information and experiences straight after seeing them;
(b) long-term memory – remembering information and experiences from a long time ago;
(c) working memory – information that has been learned, remembered and can be re-used.

Mainstream classroom the regular class in a school.

Multisensory using all the senses when learning.

Myringotomy	operation under anaesthetic...making a small hole in the ear drum so that the fluid can drain out. Often a grommet is inserted.
Oculomotor	motor movements of the eye.
One to one teaching (1:1)	when the child is given support on their own with one adult.
Onset	part of a syllable that precedes a vowel, e.g. the onset of the word 'pill' is 'p'.
Otitis media (with or without effusion)	inflammation of the middle ear. General term that encompasses all the diseases on the otitis media continuum.
Otovent	a small plastic widget with a soft balloon attached to it. The child is encouraged to blow the balloon using the nose. The idea is that opens up the eustachian tube.
Over-learning	when the child is taught the same thing several times, possibly but not necessarily in different ways.
Peer group	people of the same age.
Perception	making sense of that which is seen (visual) and heard (auditory).
Phoneme	the smallest unit of speech that distinguishes words from each other, e.g. 'pat' and 'fat'.
Phonemic awareness	the ability to be able to 'hear' specific phonemes clearly in words and/or syllables.
Phonics	an approach to the teaching of reading that emphasises letter–sound relationships.
Phonological awareness	the understanding that speech is composed of small parts which can be further broken down, e.g. words into syllables; syllables into onset and rime; appreciation of phonemes.
Phonology	sounds that make up language.
Pragmatics	how language is used in different situations and how feelings are communicated.
Rime	the part of a syllable which consists of its vowel and consonant sounds that come after it.
Self-concept/Self-esteem	how a person views themselves.
Semantics	the meaning of parts of words, words and sentences.
Specific learning difficulties	the range of conditions including at least: dyslexia, dyspraxia (especially motor difficulties), attention deficit disorder (with or without hyperactivity), dyscalculia (maths).
Syntax (grammar)	the rules for assembling words and parts of words into meaningful sentences.
Tinnitus	episodes of hearing a continuous noise inside the ear.
Tympanogram	a graph produced to show the results of a hearing test.
Tympanometry test	hearing test which shows how well the middle ear can move.
Vestibular	the vestibular system keeps tabs on the position and motion of your head in space.
Visual	things that you see.
Word bank	a storage place for learners to keep written words specific to their area of need.
Word families	a group of words that share common rhymes, e.g. pull, full, bull.

Useful contacts and materials

Organisations: Dyslexia

Adult Dyslexia Organisation
0207 924 9559 (UK)

British Dyslexia Association
www.bdadyslexia.org.uk

Council for the Registration of Schools
Teaching Dyslexic Pupils (CReSTeD)
Greygarth, Littleworth, Winchcombe,
Cheltenham GL54 5BT

Dyslexia Institute
www.dyslexia-inst.org.uk

Dyslexia Research Trust
www.dyslexic.org.uk

European Dyslexia Association
www.bedford.ac.uk/eda/

Helen Arkell Dyslexia Centre
www.arkellcentre.org.uk

Hornsby International Centre
www.hornsby.co.uk

International Academy for Research in
Learning Disabilities   www.iarld.net

International Dyslexia Association
www.interdys.org

National Association of Special
Educational Needs   www.nasen.org.uk

Peer Gordon Associates
Dr Lindsay Peer CBE, C. Psychol
www.peergordonassociates.co.uk

Dr Gavin Reid   www.gavinreid.co.uk

Organisations: Speech and Language Disorders

Afasic   www.afasic.org.uk

I CAN   www.ican.org.uk

Organisations: Attention Deficit Disorders

ADHD behaviour management
www.StressFreeADHD.com

ADHD books   www.adders.org;
www.addwarehouse.com

Attention Deficit Disorder Association
www.chadd.org;   www.add.org

The National Attention Deficit Disorder
Information Service   www.addiss.co.uk

Organisations: Dyspraxia/Developmental Co-ordination Disorders

Dyspraxia Connexion
www.dysf.fsnet.co.uk

Dyspraxia Foundation
www.dyspraxiafoundation.org.uk

Organisations: Asperger's Syndrome and Autistic Spectrum Disorders

National Autistic Society   www.nas.org.uk

www.futurehorizons-autism.com

Publishers/Products/Services

Ann Arbor   www.annarbor.co.uk

Barrington Stoke Books
www.barringtonstoke.co.uk

Crick Software   www.cricksoft.com

Crossbow Education
www.crossboweducation.com

IANSYST Ltd   *www.iansyst.co.uk*

John Wiley & Sons Ltd
www.wileyeurope.com

LDA: Literacy Resources for Special Needs
www.LDAlearning.com

Learning Works International Ltd
www.learning-works.org.uk

Lucid Research Ltd
www.lucid-research.com

Multi-Sensory Learning
www.msl-online.net

REM software company
www.r-e-m.co.uk

SEN Marketing Dyslexia and Special
Needs Bookshop   *www.sen.uk.com*

TextHelp© Computer programmes

Whurr Publishers Ltd, UK
0207 359 5979

Xavier Educational Software Ltd
www.xavier.bangor.ac.uk

Further Reading and Programmes

A Multi-Sensory Teaching System For Reading. Johnson, M., Phillips, S. and Peer, L. (1999) Manchester Metropolitan University Press.

Before Alpha: Learning Games for the Under Fives. Hornsby, B. (1996) Souvenir Press.

Developmental Dyspraxia: A Practical Manual for Parents and Professionals. Portwood, M. (1996) Durham County Council, Educational Psychology Service, County Hall, Durham.

Dyslexia: A Complete Guide for Parents. Reid, G. (2005) John Wiley and Sons: London.

Educating Children with AD(H)D: A Teacher's Manual. Cooper, P. and O'Regan, F. (2001) RoutledgeFalmer: London.

Get Ahead (Video and books on Mind Mapping©)   *www.buzan.org*

How to Identify and Support Children with Speech and Language Difficulties. Speake, J. (2003) LDA: Cambridge.

Learning Styles. Given, B. and Reid, G. (1999)   *www.dyslexiacentre.com*

Phonemic Awareness in Young Children. Adams, M., Foorman, B.R., Lundberg, I. and Beeler, T. (1998) Paul Brookes Publishing Co: Baltimore, Maryland.

Sound Linkage: An Integrated Programme for Overcoming Reading Difficulties. Hatcher, P. (1998) Whurr Publishers: London.

Sound Practice: Phonological Awareness in the Classroom. Layton, L., Deeny, K. and Upton, G. (1997) David Fulton Publishers.

Specific Learning Difficulties (Dyslexia): A Teacher's Guide. Crombie, M. (1997) Ann Arbor Publishers: Northumberland.

Star Track: Reading and Spelling. Beadle, C. and Hampshire, J. (1998) Whurr Publishers: London.

Step into Phonics: A Structured Guide for Sequential Phonics. *www.stepintophonics.com*

Supporting Children with Speech and Language Impairment and Associated Difficulties. McMinn, J. (2002) The Questions Publishing Company: Birmingham.

Teaching Reading and Spelling to Dyslexic Children. Walton, M. (1998) David Fulton Publishers: London.

The Dyslexia Handbook. British Dyslexia Association, 98, London Road, Reading, Berks RG1 5AU.

The Study Skills Handbook. Cottrell, S. (2003) Palgrave Study Guides (FE/HE).

What To Do When You Can't Learn The Times Tables. Chinn, S. (1996) Egon Publishing.

Bibliography and references

Adams, M.J. (1990) *Beginning to Read: Learning and Thinking about Print*. Cambridge, MA: MIT Press.

Brooks, R.B. (2001) Fostering Motivation, Hope and Resilience in Children with Learning Disorders. *In: Annals of Dyslexia*. Vol. 51. Baltimore: IDA.

Cunningham, A.E. (1990) Explicit versus implicit instruction in phonemic awareness. *Journal of Experimental Child Psychology*. **83**, pp.451–5.

Cunningham, A.E. and Stanovich, K. (1998) What Reading Does for the Mind. *American Educator*. **22**(182), 8–15.

Daly, K.A. (1997) Definition and Epidemiology of Otitis Media. In: J.E. Roberts, I.F. Wallace and F.W. Henderson (eds), *Otitis Media in Young Children: Medical, developmental and educational implications*. Baltimore, Maryland: Paul Brookes Publishing, pp. 14–15.

DeMarco, S. and Givens, G. (1989) Speech sound discrimination pre- and post-tympanostomy: A clinical case report. *Ear and Hearing*. **10**, pp. 64–7.

DfEE (1994) *Code of Practice on the Identification and Assessment of Special Educational Needs*. London: Department of Education.

DfES (2001) *Special Educational Needs Code of Practice*. London: Department for Education and Skills.

Disability Rights Commission (2002) EDUS, Disability Discrimination Act Part 4: A governor's guide. [online] [Accessed 20 July 2005]. Available from World Wide Web: <http//www.drc-gb.org>

Dyslexia Friendly Schools Resource Pack (2000) Reading: British Dyslexia Association.

Foorman, B., Francis, D., Novy, D. and Liberman, D. (1991) How letter–sound instruction mediates in first-grade reading and spelling. *Journal of Educational Psychology*. **83**(4), pp. 456–69.

Friel-Palti, S. and Finitzo, T. (1990) Language learning in a prospective study of otitis media with effusion in the first two years of life. *Journal of Speech and Hearing Research*. **33**, pp. 188–94.

Frith, U. (1996) Brain, Mind and Behaviour in Dyslexia. In: C. Hulme and M. Snowling (eds), *Dyslexia: Biology, Cognition and Intervention*. London: Whurr Publishers Ltd, p. 15.

Goleman, D. (1995) *Emotional Intelligence*. New York: Bantam.

Gravel, J.S. and Wallace, I.F. (1995) Early otitis media, auditory abilities and educational risk. *American Journal of Speech-Language Pathology*. **4**, pp. 89–94.

Haggard, M. (2004) Children at Risk from Delayed Ear Surgery. [Online]. [Accessed 22 August 2005]. Available from World Wide Web: <http://www.defeatingdeafness.org>

Lavoie, R. (1990) 'How Difficult can this be?' FAT City Workshop, Canada: PBS Video.

Meyer, M. and Felton, R. (1999) Repeated reading to enhance fluency: Old approaches and new directions. *Annals of Dyslexia*. **49**, pp. 283–306.

Montgomery, D. (1998) *Reversing Lower Attainment*. London:David Fulton Publishers.

Nagey, W.E., Anderson, R., Schommer, M., Scott, J.A. and Stallman, A.C. (1989) Morphological families and word recognition. *Reading Research Quarterly*. **24**, pp. 262–82.

Nicolson, R.I. and Fawcett, A.J. (1999) Developmental Dyslexia: The role of the cerebellum. *Dyslexia: An International Journal of Research and Practice*. **5**, pp. 155–77.

Office of Elementary and Secondary Education (2002) *Six dimensions of reading. Reading Excellence Act*. [online]. [Accessed 22 August 2005]. Available from World Wide Web <http://www.emsc.nysed.gov.nyc/REA.html>

Parmalee, A.H. (1993) Children's illness and normal behavioural development: The role of caregivers. *Zero to three*. **13**(4), pp. 1–9.

Peer, L. (2002) *Dyslexia, Multilingual Speakers and Otitis Media*. PhD thesis, University of Sheffield.

Peer, L. and Reid, G. (2000) *Multilingualism, Literacy and Dyslexia: A challenge for educators*. London: David Fulton Publishers.

Reid, G. and Wearmouth, J. (2002) Issues for Assessment and Planning of Teaching and Learning. In: G. Reid and J. Wearmouth (eds) *Dyslexia and Literacy: Theory and practice*. London: David Fulton Publishers. pp.151–66.

Roberts, J.E. and Wallace, I.F. (1997) *Language and Otitis Media*. In: J.E. Roberts, I.F Wallace and F.W. Henderson, *Otitis Media in Young Children*, Maryland: Paul H. Brookes Publishing Co. pp. 163–94.

Schneider, E. (1999) *Multisensory Structured Metacognitive Instruction: An approach to teaching a modern foreign language to at-risk students at an American college*. Frankfurt am Main: Peter Lang Verlag.

Schneider, E. *et al*. (1999) *Impact of English as a Foreign Language on Dyslexics: Cross cultural perspectives*. Paper presented at the International Dyslexia Association, Chicago.

Snowling, M. and Nation, K. (1997) Language, phonology and learning to read. In: C. Hulme and M. Snowling (eds), *Dyslexia: Biology, Cognition and Intervention*. London: Whurr Publishers. pp. 153–66.

Stanovich, K. (1994) Romance and Reality. *The Reading Teacher*. **47**(4), pp. 280–91.

Stanovich, K. and Siegel, L. (1994) Phenotypic performance profile of children with reading disorder regression-based test of the phonological-core variable-difference model. *Journal of Educational Psychology*. **86**(1), pp. 24–53.

Stein, J. and Walsh, V. (1997) To see but not to read: the magnocellular theory of dyslexia. *Trends in Neuroscience*. **20**, pp. 147–52.

Tallal, P., Ross, R. and Coutiss, S. (1989) Familial aggregation in specific language impairment. *Journal of Speech and Hearing Disorders*. **54**, p. 167.

Wright, A. (2004) Children at Risk from Delayed Ear Surgery. [Online]. [Accessed 22 August 2005]. Available from World Wide Web <http://www.defeatingdeafness.org>